Miracles of a Mother's Love

TRUE STORIES THAT CELEBRATE THE SPECIAL BOND BETWEEN MOTHER AND CHILD

Brad Steiger &
Sherry Hansen Steiger

ADAMS MEDIA CORPORATION
Avon, Massachusetts

Published by
Adams Media Corporation
57 Littlefield Street, Avon, MA 02322. U.S.A.
www.adamsmedia.com

ISBN: 1-58062-600-9

Printed in Canada.

J I H G F E D C B

Library of Congress Cataloging-in-Publication Data
Steiger, Brad.
Miracles of a mother's love: true stories that celebrate the special bond
between mother and child / by Brad Steiger and Sherry Hansen Steiger.
p.   cm.
ISBN 1-58062-600-9
1. Mother and Child. 2. Love, Maternal. I. Steiger, Sherry Hansen. II. Title

HQ755.85 .S737   2002
306.874'3--dc21   2001055305

This publication is designed to provide accurate and authoritative information with regard to
the subject matter covered. It is sold with the understanding that the publisher is not engaged
in rendering legal, accounting, or other professional advice. If legal advice or other expert
assistance is required, the services of a competent professional person should be sought.
—From a *Declaration of Principles* jointly adopted by a Committee of the American Bar
Association and a Committee of Publishers and Associations

While all the stories in this book are true, some of the names, dates, and places have
been changed to protect anonymity.

Illustration by Mary Cassatt/Superstock.

*This book is available at quantity discounts for bulk purchases.
For information, call 1-800-872-5627.*

Acknowledgments

We offer special thanks to the following individuals: Janice Gray Kolb, Lynda Paladin, Frank Joseph, Melissa Hansen, Carla Wills-Braden, Ph.D., June Krull, Dr. Bruce Goldberg, Bette M. Goodson, Gloria Torres, Rebecca Fouche, Hazel Olson, Clarisa Bernhardt, Ruth Johnson, Bette K. Binder, the wonderful folks at Adams, and our terrific agent, Agnes Birnbaum.

In addition, we would like to thank those who shared their stories with us, but who requested anonymity to protect their privacy. We would also like to acknowledge the love and inspiration we have received from our grandmothers, Dena, Anna, Ruth, and Nana; our miracle moms, Hazel and Lorraine; a very special aunt, Delores; a special sister, June; and the new mommies, our daughters Kari and Julie.

—BRAD and SHERRY
www.bradandsherry.com

Foreword

We believe that there is truly something special, something sacred, about the unique bond that exists between mother and child. Psychologists, philosophers, and theologians have only begun to explore the many subtle, unconscious links that exist between the expectant mother and the child that she nurtures within her womb. A growing number of medical researchers are coming to accept mothers' claims of sensing their babies in utero as far more than a romantic hypothesis.

Dr. Marshall Klaus believes that during the final months of pregnancy, a mother naturally works to bond with her unborn child. She sings and talks aloud to the child within her womb because she *knows* that the child hears and responds with synchronous body movements.

Dr. Klaus portrays the first hour after birth as the most critical time in human life: "For now the bond between mother and child is established in strange, mysterious and unfathomable ways. Anyone else around literally gets caught in the magnetic fields of attraction weaving back and forth. The self has divided and reunites with the self. The hologram part starts immediately moving into and reflecting the whole."

Further describing the mystical process of mother-child bonding, Dr. Klaus says that it is as if the mother possesses a kind of "magical glue" that is designed to seal the new infant right into her.

Dr. David Cheek agrees that the first moments of life are crucial to the intense rapport that occurs between mother and child. He has collected hundreds of cases in which extraordinary acts of both predelivery and postdelivery communication could be recalled in adult life.

Dr. Stanley Krippner, who served as the director of the William C. Menninger Dream Laboratory at Maimonides Medical Center in Brooklyn, New York, found many instances of a telepathic link between expectant mothers and their unborn children. And who can deny that this psychic link continues to exist between mother and child throughout their lifetimes?

A mother's first act of courage on behalf of her infant is to enter, as it were, the valley of the shadow of death, and give her baby life at risk of losing her own. In addition, the selfless heroism of mothers protecting their young is legendary. E. H. Chapin commented that the majesty of a mother's love "shrinks not where man cowers, and grows stronger where man faints." Chapin must have had in mind such women as Pam Prier-Steward and Candace Franklin.

Pam Prier-Steward of Park Hills, Missouri, stopped to admire the mighty Mississippi River along with her husband, Shelby, and their four kids, including two-year-old Kira. Pam had left Kira alone in the car for just a second or two, but it was long enough for the baby to somehow knock the car's gear lever into neutral.

As Pam and the rest of the family watched in horror, Kira and their automobile plunged into the river at a spot especially noted for its treacherous, churning currents. Pam, a five-foot-two, eighty-three-pound woman who barely knew how to swim, somehow found the strength and courage to battle the raging river. Plunging into the swirling waters, she was miraculously able to pull her daughter from within the car as it sank toward the murky bottom, 200 feet below.

Candace Franklin of Hartford, Connecticut, had just finished changing a tire on her car when a thug jumped into the driver's seat and drove off. Candace's three-year-old daughter and three-month-old son were strapped in their car seats.

Determined to stop the carjacker, Candace threw her body in the way so he could not shut the door, and she hung on with all the strength of her "mother's magical glue," refusing to release her hold even though she was being dragged across the pavement. The thief jerked the wheel back and forth, trying to shake Candace loose, but she held on for 200 feet until she managed to grab the stick shift and slam it into park. Then she jumped on the hoodlum and began pummeling him with her fists. She kept pounding him until someone in the crowd that had gathered pulled her off and turned the carjacker over to the police.

Candace suffered cuts and scratches from her toes to her thighs, and her knees looked like raw hamburger from being dragged on the asphalt, but her powerful maternal love enabled her to hang on to the car door so she could save her babies.

And then there are those mysterious occurrences when a mother sees no visible sign of threat or danger to her child, but somehow *knows* she must act to help or even to save her dear one's life.

Twenty-eight-year-old Jean Dickinson of Chicago felt a sudden urge to pick up her two-year-old daughter from her indoor swing and carry her over to the couch. Seconds later, a thirty-pound chunk of ice crashed through the roof of their home, ripped a coffee-table-sized hole in their ceiling, and smashed the child's swing to pieces. FAA inspectors later said that the ice chunk could have come from a jet airplane. Jean only knows for certain that a "funny feeling" enabled her to save her daughter's life.

Then, there was the day when Jana Murphy of a Boston suburb had more than a "funny" feeling in her stomach. All of a sudden, she had extreme feelings of uneasiness and nausea that she somehow *knew* were related to her nine-year-old daughter, Vanessa, who was at school. Although Vanessa had looked well when she left that morning, it was as if Jana could actually hear her little daughter saying, "Mommy, please come and get me. I'm really, really sick." Then waves of nausea would hit her again.

Jana left work and drove to the elementary school where Vanessa was a pupil. She was not surprised to find that her daughter was not in class but had been sent to the nurse's office, complaining of feeling ill and nauseated. A few minutes later as Jana entered the office, she found the nurse trying to call her at her work number. When both the astonished nurse and Vanessa wondered how Jana knew to come to school to get her daughter, she could respond only by saying that mothers just *know* when their children need them.

I, Sherry will share personal accounts of the many "funny feelings" that I have experienced that have, on one occasion, saved my children from the destructive force a tornado, and, in another situation, averted their involvement in the deadly impact of an automobile accident. And together we will present remarkable stories of how, in ways that our sciences cannot yet define, loving mothers had within them the ability to receive knowledge about their children, even at great distances.

Dr. Louisa E. Rhine, who conducted the famous "ESP Lab" at Duke University, researched hundreds of cases of mother-child telepathy and clairvoyance.

Such reports, which seemingly lie beyond the parameters of normal perception, confirm again and again the strange, mysterious, and unfathomable bond between mother and child.

And yet there is a connection between mother and child that far transcends "woman's intuition" or the farthest reaches of the paranormal. It has been said that a mother's love is the golden link that binds us to God by giving us an earthly example of the kind of unconditional love we might expect in Heaven.

As William Makepeace Thackeray once expressed it, "Mother is the name for God in the lips and hearts of little children."

Or in the words of that old Jewish saying, "God could not be everywhere, and therefore he made mothers."

If, as we believe, love is the greatest power in the universe, then a mother's love is one aspect of that marvelous cosmic energy that emanates directly from an all-loving source.

In *Miracles of a Mother's Love*, we shall present many inspirational stories of mothers whose sacred bond with their children allowed them to work miracles. In some instances, the power of their love wouldn't even let death itself prevent them from coming to their child's aid in times of crisis.

—SHERRY HANSEN STEIGER
—BRAD STEIGER
Forest City, Iowa
July 2001

*T*his is a story about how the gift of a mother's love saved the lives of another mother's children. And how a very good, very obedient son was the instrument of deliverance.

Twenty-nine-year-old Alex Davis was riding with his mother, Ann, near their home in Cleveland, Ohio, when they saw a two-story house engulfed in flames. Good neighbors and citizens, the Davises pulled over to see if they could be of any help.

A desperate Theresa Montgomery, one of the tenants, told Alex and his mother that her five babies, together with teenager Shadina Cummings, were still inside the blazing inferno.

The pleas of the anguished mother touched Ann Davis deeply. Perhaps her son, Alex, would save the children. Of course she was concerned for the safety of her own son, but she simply could not bear to think of those six children dying in the flames.

Alex could actually see some of the children standing at the second floor windows. He offered to run into the house, race up the stairs, and carry the children to safety, even though Theresa informed him that the stairs were on fire.

Alex took a deep breath, pulled his hooded coat over his head, and without another moment's hesitation, ran into the flaming building.

Aware that smoke inhalation could kill him quicker than the fire, Alex dodged the flames as he raced up the burning stairs. Once on the second floor, he got down on all fours and crawled around in the billowing clouds of smoke, groping for the children. When he touched the smallest ones, he pulled them into his arms, and told the older ones to follow him carefully down the stairs.

"The heat and smoke were choking us and flaming parts of the house were falling all around us," Alex later reported, "but we got out."

When Alex staggered out of the hellish inferno with

the children in his arms, neighbors cheered. Theresa Montgomery sobbed gratefully as she took count of her babies. Alex had saved the lives of four of her children, ages two to seven, and thirteen-year-old Shadina Cummings—but Theresa's ten-month-old baby, Walter, was still somewhere inside the fast-collapsing, flame-consumed house.

"Go back," a somber Ann Davis told her son. "You have to go back and save Baby Walter."

This time the flames and the smoke were much worse. Somehow Alex once again managed to climb the burning stairs to the second floor. But once he had achieved that seemingly impossible goal, he found that he was blinded by smoke.

For moments that seemed like tortured hours, Alex crawled around from room to room until at last his searching fingers felt what seemed to be a couch—then what he believed to be a diaper. And then they closed around what he knew for certain was a baby's leg.

Alex could tell that little Walter was unconscious but still alive. He carefully placed the infant inside his coat and braced himself for another run down the fiery stairs.

Once again, Alex Davis scored a touchdown of the most heroic kind. He had saved all six children in the house from a terrible death by fire.

None of the children were injured. Paramedics

quickly revived Baby Walter with oxygen, and Alex himself suffered only minor burns.

Jonathan Parries of the Cleveland Fire Department declared Alex Davis a bona fide hero and stated that it was certain that those six children would have died without his selfless actions.

Alex responded that he had no choice but to do as he did. Those people were his neighbors. "And besides," he added, "my mother told me to!"

*A*nita Mayer was experiencing a great deal of pain as she slowed her car and prepared to turn into a driveway leading to the hospital. Her upper right arm and shoulder had been giving her trouble for a couple of weeks, and specialists at the hospital had run some tests and taken X-rays to determine whether she had fractured a bone or pulled a tendon. On that afternoon in June 1994, Connie, Anita's four-year-old daughter, was beside her, securely fastened in the child's safety seat in the family's second car, a vintage 1982 automobile.

"I promised Connie that Mommy would just be a few minutes talking with the doctors," Anita said. "I told her that if she was very good while we waited for the doctors to look at Mommy's X-rays, we could stop for some ice cream on the way home."

Then, just as she turned into the driveway, a freak accident occurred. Because of her handicapped right arm, Anita was unable to negotiate the turn into the drive, and struck the curb with considerable force. The car door on the driver's side suddenly swung open, and she fell out onto the rough pavement.

"I had warned my husband, Luke, about the door on that old car for months," Anita said. "The latch never seemed to catch the way it should. I told him I was afraid that sometime the door might fly open when one of us was driving on the freeway and something might fall out. I didn't imagine it might be me. Of course I had my seat belt on, but for some reason it didn't keep me in the car. The buckle just seemed to pop open, and I went sprawling out on the pavement, skinning my elbows, my knees, and my forehead."

But far worse than the injuries she sustained was the knowledge that little Connie was still buckled into her child's safety seat—and now the runaway car was headed toward the lake behind the hospital!

Anita had no idea of the depth of the lake, but the

fact that it was a popular place for swimming and rowing indicated that it had to be at least several feet deep. Deep enough to engulf her automobile and Connie.

Anita got unsteadily to her feet. She called for help, but, as fate would have it, there was no one at that moment outside the hospital or in the parking lot. There was no time to run inside and try to explain to nurses at a crowded admittance desk that her daughter was in a runaway car headed toward the lake.

There was nothing for her to do but to run after the car—and pray.

"I knew that somehow it was up to me—and to God—to save Connie," Anita said. "It didn't matter that I could barely lift my right arm and that I was all banged up and bloody. From somewhere, I knew that I must find the strength to save my baby."

The car hit a park bench, which slowed its descent toward the lake. Anita felt her pounding heart surge with hope, and she prayed that the bench would delay the car long enough for her to catch up with it and grab Connie from the safety seat.

But the bench was not permanently anchored into the cement slab on which it rested, and the heavy car easily ploughed it aside and rolled on into the lake.

"I hoped that it might float," Anita recalled. "But that old car began to sink like a rock."

As she splashed into the lake water, Anita screamed at Connie to get out of the car.

"She had already taken some swimming lessons," Anita said. "I knew she could swim. But I could see her crying in panic, tugging at the belt that held her fast in her car seat. The car suddenly entered a deeper area of the lake, and the water was now at window level. All I could think of at that moment was that my baby was going to drown."

Desperately, Anita swam toward the car. Its momentum had carried it many yards from the shore, and from her perspective it would soon be completely under water.

"I got close enough to see Connie standing at the window," Anita said. "She had managed to free herself from the car seat and to lower the window, but the force of the water rushing into the car was holding her back."

Anita screamed in horror as the car dipped deeper into the lake, and she could see the fear in her daughter's eyes as she tried to keep her little chin above the water.

"Then a glorious miracle occurred," Anita said. "Just as it seemed the car was almost completely under the water, taking Connie with it, I saw clearly the outline of a glowing hand, a huge glowing hand, move under the car. As I watched in wonder, the hand of an angel seemed to lift the car far enough above the water so I could reach in the window and pull Connie free. I had no sooner managed to pull her to safety when the car sank completely and disappeared into the murky waters of the deepest part of the lake."

Sobbing, holding Connie tight with her painful right arm, Anita began to swim back toward shore, speaking words of comfort to calm her daughter's fears. "It's all right now, honey. Mommy's got you. You're going to be okay."

And then Anita became aware of a man beside her in the water. "At last, a number of people had witnessed our plight from the hospital windows, and there were three men in the lake to take Connie from me and to help me back to shore," she said.

"For the rest of my life, I will always know that God heard my desperate plea for help and sent an angel to lift the car out of the water long enough for me to pull Connie to safety. Our daughter is now twelve years old, and every wonderful day that we share together reminds me how blessed we are that God answered my prayer to spare her life."

*S*andra O'Donnell, who lives in a Minneapolis suburb, remembered those anxious days in August 1990 when she was awaiting the delivery of her second child. Her first baby had died at birth, and she prayed that this time God would allow the tiny life within her womb to emerge safely into the world.

A week before she was due, she awakened one morning to find that she could not see out of one eye.

"I shook my husband, Garry, awake, and I told him that I could see only whiteness with my left eye.

He telephoned Dr. Mason, our family physician, and within an hour or so we were in his office."

Dr. Mason could not explain Sandra's sudden loss of vision. He readily admitted that its cause lay beyond his expertise. He suggested that it might go away in a day or two, but if it did not, he would recommend an eye specialist.

"I wondered if the sudden loss of my vision might not be psychosomatic," Sandra O'Donnell admitted. "Perhaps I could not bear to 'see' another of my children born dead. I spent two worried days and sleepless nights until I decided to see a specialist and learn his opinion about my condition."

Dr. Mason arranged an appointment with Dr. Graef, who examined Sandra extensively before discovering that a pinched blood vessel was cutting off circulation to the eye. He stated his analysis firmly: If something was not done immediately, she risked permanent blindness in her left eye.

"As if I was not worried enough about the safe delivery of my baby in just a few days, I now had the grim specter of blindness in one eye to raise my stress levels," she said.

Dr. Graef advised Sandra to check into the hospital to receive a series of typhoid fever shots. It was his medical opinion that the inoculations would raise her temperature and open the constricted blood vessel.

"Although Garry thought that we should go at once to the hospital for the shots, my first thought was of our unborn child," Sandra said. "Even though Dr. Graef kept trying to convince me that the induced fever would in no way harm the baby, I was unable to accept his assurances. I wanted to take no chances of any kind that might in any way threaten our child's well-being, and I could not be convinced that this kind of 'fever therapy' would not threaten an unborn baby. I left Dr. Graef's office declaring that I would rather lose the sight in my left eye than risk the loss of my child."

Sandra recalled that she went to bed quite late that night. Although Garry had agreed that the decision to reject Dr. Graef's advice was hers to make, they still managed to get into an argument when he begged her to reconsider the almost certain risk to her eyesight.

"Sometime during the night, I had this wonderful dream," she said. "I saw myself floating on fluffy white clouds until I stood before a great golden door in the heavens. I opened the door and saw before me a beautiful green meadow with a dazzling array of multicolored flowers.

"I had not walked for long in the glorious meadow when I saw a ray of golden light streak down from the heavens—and on the ray of light there descended a large white dove with a beautiful golden-haired baby boy riding on its back. The child's large blue eyes looked up at me with such great love, and I heard a voice that seemed to emanate from the dove, saying, 'Behold, thy son. Have no fears. Follow the feelings of your heart.'"

Sandra O'Donnell awakened from the dream greatly at peace. She was certain that she had received a sign that her child would be born safely and without incident.

"I truly had a new hope and faith," she said. "I no longer felt like crying, and the old fears were gone. Somehow I knew that whatever would happen with my eyesight would be part of a larger plan. I would follow my inner feelings and do nothing to jeopardize my baby's well-being."

On November 20, 1990, Kevin O'Donnell was born alive and healthy. "He had curly blond hair and large blue eyes," Sandra said. "The doctors said that he was completely sound of body.

"And to add to my great joy, I could see clearly once again with my left eye!

"Later, when Dr. Graef examined me, he theorized that the rigors of childbirth must have somehow unkinked the blood vessel. When he asked why I had been so willing to take a chance with my eyesight, I smiled and said that a big white birdie had told me that everything would be all right."

*N*ever to be under-
estimated is the power
of a mother's love.

The birth had been so sudden and unexpected that
the doctor had not yet arrived in the delivery room.
But when the nurses took her baby to a nearby table to
check for vital signs, Deborah Goodwin experienced a
moment of great concern. She could not hear her baby
crying. And the nurses were too quiet.

Then, a nurse held one of Deborah's hands and
sadly informed her that her premature baby had been
born dead. With tears streaming down her face,

Deborah asked to see the baby, to hold it. After the nurses had cleaned up the lifeless form, they brought it to the young mother.

Deborah reached out to take the still, tiny form of the girl whom she had named Taryn. She wanted to embrace the daughter she would never get to know for at least a few moments before she said goodbye.

Deborah and her husband, Brian, had been fearful of a tragic end to her pregnancy when in the twenty-second week she began to bleed. Doctors warned the Goodwins, who reside in Courtenay, British Columbia, that Deborah's life was in danger, as well as the child within her womb, but the young mother, who also had a four-year-old son, resolved to direct all her energy toward saving Taryn.

Deborah was rushed by helicopter to Victoria General Hospital, 150 miles from their home, and within one week's time she was given six transfusions, while losing half of her own blood. After carefully assessing the situation, doctors grimly pronounced that Deborah's chances of saving her baby would be 0 to 5 percent.

At eight in the morning on October 29, 1993, Deborah went into labor. The nurses wheeled her to the delivery room, but they didn't anticipate the baby for at least another two hours, so the doctor had not been called.

And then, suddenly, Deborah began giving birth, but the tiny premature baby had been born dead. She had weighed slightly more than a pound and was only eleven and a half inches long.

As the saddened nurse placed the body of Taryn in her arms, Deborah remembers that she felt a great peace come over her. She understood that there was a plan for everything in God's universe and a reason for every action that He took. She thanked God for allowing her to be able to hold her child and to see her lovely face.

It was at that moment that the miracle occurred.

Although Taryn Goodwin had been outside of her mother's womb for at least five minutes and had exhibited absolutely no signs of life, at the very second that Deborah completed her prayer of acceptance of God's will, Taryn's eyes opened wide and stared right at her. And then she raised her arms.

Deborah Goodwin felt shivers run down her spine, and she screamed out the joyous news that her baby was alive.

The nurses, awestruck and dumbfounded, rushed the premature infant into the special care nursery, where they set about applying their medical skills and knowledge to help tiny Taryn maintain her tenuous hold on life.

Two hours later, Brian Goodwin arrived at the

hospital, not knowing what to expect about the condition of both his wife and their unborn child. While Deborah had been transported the 150 miles by helicopter, Brian had been left to drive to Victoria General Hospital by car.

When he walked into the recovery room and saw his wife's radiant smile and learned that their new daughter was alive, he "couldn't stop the tears from flowing."

Tiny Taryn was placed in an incubator and had to stay at the hospital for ninety-nine days before her parents were able to take her home with them. Head nurse Wendy Amos, who had assisted in the birth, told a reporter that Taryn was a miracle baby. "There is no medical explanation for why she came to life in the arms of her loving mother. Now at sixteen pounds, Taryn is a totally healthy child [who will] grow up normal in every way."

I don't think of my relationship with my mother as being particularly close or deep—none of those sweet exchanges I hear about from daughters who have become best friends with their moms.

I grew up; married David Paladin, the well-known Navajo painter; and moved to another state. Through the years, I kept in touch with Mother with short phone calls, exchanging the usual surface pleasantries. Our annual visits were filled with sightseeing, eating, and playing cards. I had my life; she had hers. My interests and activities were miles apart from hers. In short, we had nothing in common.

Then, one day, through a strange set of circumstances, my mother rearranged her travel plans to
visit us for the holidays earlier than she had originally
planned. Since she was unable to stay for Christmas,
we had our little celebration the day she arrived. David
prepared a delicious dinner, and we exchanged gifts in
the living room near the Christmas tree, gaily festooned
with David's handmade ornaments, surrounded by his
paintings that hung on the walls. We were all so happy
that day. Later, declining to join Mother and me in a
game of cards, David went off to the bedroom, claiming
that he needed to lie down. Three hours later, he was
dead from a heart attack.

Stunned, I went with David in the ambulance to the
hospital, while Mother drove there separately to meet
me. After his death, she was there to drive me home. I
struggled with the numbness and shock of being thrust
into a foreign reality—grateful that Mother was there for
me. Like a midwife, she eased the pain of my entry into a
new life.

After she had returned to her home a couple of days
later, I was musing about the sequence of events. What a
strange coincidence that Mother would show up on the
day that David died. Then I remembered that Mother
had been with me the day that I met David as we toured
the Southwest. Mother was there the day I met David,

and she was there the day my life with him ended.

As a result of that experience, something deepened between us or changed in the undercurrent that binds mothers and daughters together. To me, the mother-daughter relationship is a mystery because it cannot be explained with words. It is a part of our essential selves—of who we are, together and separately.

I know that although there doesn't appear to be much happening between Mother and me on the surface, there is a deeper connection that I can't deny. Since this realization, I have come to honor my mother and the strange bit of magic she carries through my life. I particularly honor her intuition, and that place deep within her that just "knows."

—LYNDA PALADIN

*I*n 1987, I bought a new Honda Civic. In it, I piled two ice-augers, hammers, saws, chisels, a twelve-volt battery, cables, an underwater lighting system, lead weights, and a large wooden box fitted with angled mirrors at both ends. The device was an inverted periscope that would allow me to look beneath the body of water I was investigating at the time.

Since March, I had been trying, unsuccessfully, to find the "lost pyramids" alleged to stand at the bottom of Wisconsin's Rock Lake, located about 60 miles west of

Milwaukee. Scuba dives from spring through summer were mostly frustrated by poor subsurface visibility. I returned to the lake during late December in the hope of sinking a periscope beneath the ice for a look around through what I assumed would be clearer water conditions, thus affording us a glimpse of a drowned structure.

A ferocious blizzard that had ended only days before our outing, dropped Wisconsin into below-zero temperatures. When Steve Dempsey, the periscope's inventor, and I reached Rock Lake, it resembled the Antarctic. The surface had been transformed into a snow-burdened ice cap, over which we laboriously hauled our ponderous gear to a spot above the suspected location of a sunken pyramid.

The mile-plus-long trek through snow and ice from the car parked back at the lakeshore was more arduous than we anticipated. So, I gunned my new Honda out onto the ice cap, to our periscope site. I had never done anything of the kind before. My decision was entirely spontaneous. And the drive seemed weird in the extreme, as I recalled how, just a few months before, we passed over this same stretch of lake in a pontoon boat.

I parked near Steve, and he helped me unload the rest of our equipment from the hatchback. Glancing down, we could see water running free beneath a foot of translucent ice. Even so, the ice cap seemed firm, and I comforted myself with the knowledge that, during World War II, the Red Army had successfully laid railroad tracks over frozen lakes that supported the passage of whole troop trains.

But I suddenly experienced a convulsion of fear, and unaccountably looked at my wristwatch—it was one o'clock—then at the Honda. Almost as though it were actually happening, I envisioned ice breaking open under the front of my car, which plunged suddenly with a great splash into the frigid water, utterly disappearing into the black depths of Rock Lake.

Without a word of explanation to Steve, I jumped behind the wheel, switched on the ignition, and drove across the lake as fast as possible, raising a cloud of snow behind me. The ice cap never gave any indication of cracking.

When my new Honda was parked safely on shore again, I walked back to my somewhat bewildered colleague. Our best efforts that day came to nothing, chiefly because the lake water was not as clear as we had expected, allowing us no better visibility than earlier in the year.

Three hours and 150 miles later, I visited with my mother, Virginia, to tell her about our strenuous, but somewhat comical, adventure. But as I entered her room, I noticed at once that she seemed upset. "Oh, Frank, I'm so glad you're all right," she said. "I was sitting here this afternoon, doing my crossword puzzle, when a terrible picture suddenly came into my head out of nowhere. I saw your new car break through the ice on Rock Lake, and sink all the way to the bottom. I prayed you were all right."

Mother remembered noticing the time of her vision: 1:00. Curiously, she envisioned the back end of the Honda falling through the ice, while I saw it going down by the front. In any case, our synchronicity was one of many we had shared since I was a boy, and it helped to reaffirm that imperishable, psychic bond between mother and child.

—FRANK JOSEPH, author of
*The Lost Pyramids of Rock Lake:
Wisconsin's Sunken Civilization*

On a cold January night in 1988, Julia Cantrell, thirteen, of southern Missouri sat vigil with her mother, Ida, as Buddy, Julia's four-year-old brother, lay in a coma. The doctors at Memorial Hospital had told them it was unlikely that Buddy would live through the night.

"Sister," her mother said in a voice that was warped with emotion, "I have been praying for your little brother's life for hours now. You've got to join me in prayer, and we just have to pray him through this terrible time. Doctors aren't always right. And God can always work a miracle."

"I have been praying, Momma," Julia assured her mother. "I've asked God to please forgive anything wicked or nasty that I have ever done and to please, please not punish little Buddy for anything that I did."

For the first time that evening Julia saw a flicker of a smile tug at her mother's lips. "Child, what wicked or nasty thing have you ever done? You're a good girl, and your prayers are going to touch God's heart."

"I just wish Daddy was here to pray with us," Julia said. "He can make such big, powerful prayers."

"You know that he is praying himself hoarse in that big old truck of his," her mother told her. "And you know that he will be here just as fast as that old rig will carry him. Come now, let us bend our knees, bow our heads, and pray together for little Buddy."

The two of them got down on their knees beside Buddy's hospital bed and folded their hands. Ida Cantrell led them in the Lord's Prayer and the Twenty-third Psalm, and then began an earnest, heartfelt, personal prayer of supplication.

About 4:45 A.M., a tall nurse with a warm smile walked into the hospital room, removed Buddy's covers, gave him an injection, then gently stroked his face.

As the nurse turned to walk away, she touched Julia softly on the shoulder and told her not to give up hope.

She reached into a pocket and gave Julia a handkerchief to dry her tears.

Miraculously, a short time later, Buddy began to cry. He had emerged safely from his coma.

"Praise the Lord, the angels, and all the saints in heaven!" Ida offered her thanks through her tears of joy.

Lonnie Cantrell, hollow-eyed from lack of sleep and from pushing his rig far more miles a day than he should have, arrived just in time to join his wife and daughter in fervent prayers of thanksgiving.

The doctors were amazed at the child's subsequent rapid recovery, and three days later Buddy was discharged.

As the family was leaving the hospital, Julia wished to thank the kind nurse and return the handkerchief that she had loaned her.

The soft linen bore the monogram "MAT," but the head nurse said that none of the nursing staff had such initials.

And when they checked Buddy's records, there was no indication that any nurse had visited him at 4:45 A.M. — and no injection of any kind had been authorized by the doctors.

The Cantrell family's confusion was resolved when a cleaning lady overheard their questions and informed them that a young nurse named Mary Ann Taggert had been killed in a car wreck as she left the hospital many years ago. Mary Ann had dreamed of becoming a doctor, and many of the older members of the hospital staff believed that her spirit lived on by helping very sick children.

"I can't swear that I know the whole truth of what happened," Julia Cantrell said. "But my folks and I like to believe that Momma's prayers touched God's heart. We like to think that maybe He permitted the spirit of Mary Ann, the loving, caring nurse, to come back and help Buddy pull through. Momma always says that prayer really can move mountains."

*S*ome women long to be mothers, having dreamt about the experience since they were children. I was one such little girl, and as an only—and often lonely—child, I dreamt and believed that one day I would be blessed with six children.

But some women find it more difficult to actually become a mother, and when they are eventually able to achieve this precious state, they are exceptional gifts to their children. I knew such a mother. She was mine.

My mother, Violet M. Gray, was loving, capable, and creative. She had a generous and giving heart, always reaching out to others. During World War II, she worked extensively for the Red Cross, knitting scarves, hats, long helmet liners, and gloves for our boys in the service. As a little girl, I, too, knitted some of these necessities with guidance from my mother as she worked on her own knitting. She was also a Sunday School teacher to a group of young girls in our Methodist Church, and I witnessed their love for her and the joy she had in teaching them, for she often invited them to our home and took them on trips with my dad's help.

In addition to all of the above, she was the manager of a large costume jewelry store in Philadelphia. My mother spent hours of her own time creating jewelry to be sold at benefits that helped many causes. She donated all the money generated from the sale of the jewelry to the cause at hand, keeping nothing for herself. She was loved by all her customers and by all with whom she worked. I saw great evidence of this.

She was the best mother that she was capable of being during those growing-up years from infancy to the time that I turned twenty-one and married. But my childhood and teen years were darkly shadowed by her personal fears and problems. Whenever I was punished for an infraction of her strict code of behavior, she would impose a silence of hours, days, or weeks upon me. To be forced to live in silence by the mother I loved, and to have to endure these mute episodes for very long periods of time, created deep feelings of unworthiness and inferiority within me. Though my dad was loving and kind, he simply could not change Mother's peculiar method of discipline. He thought that her problems might stem from her being the youngest of nine children of Irish immigrants, and he eventually gave up trying to help.

But herein begins the miraculous part of our relationship, and it leaves me amazed to this day. Two weeks after I turned twenty-one, I married, and that same weekend I left for San Diego with my new husband, Bob. He was in the Navy, and following our wedding in Philadelphia, he was required to return to California for the next eight months.

Just as my life changed at that time through marriage, so did my relationship with my mother. Immediately after I left, she called me to apologize for all the painful incidents of my growing-up years. I repeatedly had to assure her of my forgiveness, but she called again and again until she was at last able to accept it and forgive herself. I also asked forgiveness for anything I did to hurt her. I was so happy to have my mother back. She and Dad came to visit us in San Diego, and I was able to experience the change in her firsthand.

In fact, from the time I turned twenty-one until the day she died many years later, she was the most loving and generous and precious mother and grandmother.

Our six children knew her as a wonderful grandmother who loved them and who was part of their lives. Though she continued to work in the jewelry store, she came every Thursday to visit us. It was her day off, and she would arrive early in the morning, giving over the entire day to me to do as I pleased while she helped me. Sometimes she would clean or fix things in the house that needed attention. Other times we would take which-ever children were not yet in school and go shopping. Then, she would treat us to lunch in a restaurant.

Whatever was needed, she was there. She did not just use words to say she was sorry—she showed me by her actions and by the way she treated me and the members of our growing family with great love and respect. She loved my husband as if he were her own son.

Mother had truly experienced a spiritual conversion to the highest and most loving degree, and I know that she had been touched by God. I was so grateful to have her in my life in this incredible new way. The loving woman who created jewelry for others became a shining jewel to me.

Just six years ago, I discovered a small collection of Mother's belongings in a closet on the third floor of our former home in Jenkintown, Pennsylvania. After my parents' sudden deaths in 1977 and 1978, the boxes must have been tucked away to go over later, as were many of their belongings. I did not remember this particular collection of papers, envelopes, and photos stored in an old blue dishpan. It was a major discovery and, ultimately, incredibly moving.

Among these personal things I found a piece of torn paper all creased and folded unevenly. It looked like trash. But unfolding it carefully, I found within a treasure.

Here before me in her hasty writing was a poem she had written about me and my first baby. I believed that day that from "somewhere over the rainbow," my very colorful (and she was) mother had given me a gift more priceless than the pot of gold. My love for her reaches to beyond the stars, and I know that she knows this.

Mother
by Violet M. Gray

Janice Elizabeth
My lucky star—this little girl
So peaceful in her bed,
With big blue eyes and curly hair
And dimpled cheeks so red.
She grasped my little finger

With her tiny slender hand
And held it tight in greeting
Long . . . that I would understand.
Her names are Janice and Elizabeth
And echo in my heart
Of golden promise
That we'll never be apart.
And so I think in years to come
That she will always be—
As on the day that she arrived
My lucky star to me.
And now my Daughter's tiny tot
My little June Leslie who
Just like her mother long ago
Now holds my finger too.

Perhaps the real miracle of this story is recognizing that it is never too late. We can change and turn things around completely, if we but try. With effort, any failed relationship can become a wonderful one, filled with happiness and vibrant love if all involved are willing to forgive and change. God truly works in mysterious ways, His wonders to perform.

—JANICE GRAY KOLB,
author of *The Enchantment of Writing*

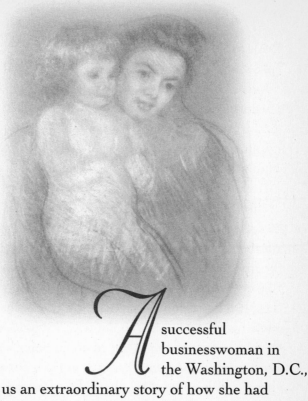

A successful businesswoman in the Washington, D.C., area told us an extraordinary story of how she had managed to locate her missing daughter and bring her to the hospital just in time to save her from overdosing on drugs.

"Janet had been going through a rebellious period. She had been experimenting with recreational drugs in a very reckless manner," Ava Johanneson said. "We had had one violent quarrel after another over her irresponsible lifestyle, and one night Janet just left the house and disappeared."

Three months went by, and the frantic mother had no idea where her eighteen-year-old daughter had vanished to.

"I had not heard one word from her," Ava said. "The police had been unable to find a single clue to her whereabouts. I didn't even know if she was alive or dead. It was a terrible, heartbreaking situation for a mother to be in."

Ava telephoned her ex-husband on the West Coast, hoping that Janet might have gone there to try the California lifestyle, but he had had no word from their daughter either.

"I can't tell you how miserable I felt," Ava said. "If only I had known *where* Janet was, I would have telephoned her and begged her to come home so that we could work things out."

Ava is legally blind. Only by holding papers at a certain angle and moving them close to her thick-lensed eyeglasses can she read the numerous documents relevant to her prosperous manufacturing business.

One day as she sat in her office thinking things could not get much worse, Ava accidentally knocked her glasses off her desk—and subsequently stepped on them, smashing them as she searched for them. With a sinking feeling, she realized that her one remaining pair of glasses was in her dressing room at home.

"It was at that moment that the telephone rang," Ava said. "My secretary said it was someone who insisted on speaking only to me. I answered and heard only one word—'Momma'—and the line went dead. I knew that it was my Janet and that she was very ill and needed me at once!"

At first it seemed like cruel fate. She had not heard from Janet in months, and now only a one-word telephone call. Where was she? Was she calling from a faraway city?

No. Ava felt in her mother's heart that the call had come from the city. But where?

And then an incredible miracle occurred. Ava suddenly had a clear mental image of a row of shoddy apartment buildings bordering the city's slum area. As she focused on the remarkable photograph in her mind, she suddenly knew that she could find the very room from which her daughter had telephoned.

After all these months of anxiety, sleepless nights, worrying about Janet, Ava now *knew* where she was— but she had just smashed her glasses and couldn't see a thing without them. How could she drive to her daughter's side in time to help her? It was useless to call for help—she would only waste time explaining how she knew where Janet was.

And then Ava experienced another miracle—she could see!

"I picked up a city map from my bookcase," she said. "After years and years of eyesight so bad I was declared legally blind, I could now read even the smallest print on the map. And then I knew exactly where Janet was. My eyes focused on one particular address. In my mind I could see an apartment, and I could clearly see my daughter lying unconscious beside the telephone."

Amazingly, Ava, who normally had great difficulty seeing well enough to drive even with her prescription eyeglasses, got into her automobile and drove unerringly through the large city to the exact address that she had envisioned. She could now see everything as clearly as though she had 20/20 vision. Not even the smallest lettering on sign posts presented the slightest difficulty. It was as if she once again possessed the sharp and clear vision of her childhood.

Once she determined that her daughter did, indeed, reside in an apartment at that address, she persuaded the superintendent to allow her access and to call an ambulance.

"I held Janet's head in my lap until the ambulance arrived," Ava said. "She was completely unconscious and had no awareness of my presence. Thank God, I was in time."

It was later apparent to investigators that Janet had accidentally overdosed on drugs, realized her error, then desperately reached out for her mother's unconditional love by attempting a telephone call for help before she lapsed into unconsciousness.

But what will never be explained is how Ava was able immediately to know the exact whereabouts of the daughter from whom she had received no communication at all for many months—and how, though legally blind, she was able to see perfectly well to drive through heavy traffic to an address that was previously unknown to her.

Then, as soon as the paramedics and police arrived and she was certain that Janet was safe and would be cared for by medical professionals, Ava's wonderfully clear vision left her as suddenly as it had mysteriously come upon her. She knew that without her special prescription eyeglasses, it would once again be impossible for her to negotiate the city streets that she had just minutes before traveled so effortlessly, and she asked a police officer to drive her home.

The only explanation possible to Ava and to Janet, who now works in her mother's business, is that sometimes a mother's love can work miracles.

A woman from New Jersey acquired the knack of slipping out of and back into her physical body during a series of childhood illnesses. Later in life, when Susan became a mother, she many times employed this unique method to keep tabs on her kids, Bruce, Keith, and Carol.

"When I was around nine and ten, it seemed as though I suffered through one darned bug after another—chicken pox, measles, mumps, scarlet fever, sinusitis," she said. "In fourth grade, I missed two months of school, and I had to try to keep up with the

rest of my class by doing my homework from my bed.
I started getting behind, and I really got frustrated. I
was so tired of lying there in bed. More than anything
else in the world I wanted to be back in school."

Susan remembered that the first time she had an
out-of-body experience, she had simply lain in bed one
morning and concentrated "with all her might" on
going to school.

"In my mind, I went through all the motions, just as
if I were physically getting ready to go to school. In my
head I got dressed, ate breakfast, and walked to school.
I didn't neglect a single detail, right down to brushing
my teeth and putting ribbons in my pigtails. Mentally,
I completely re-created a typical morning's preparation
and journey to the school building.

"Then a kind of cloud seemed to pass before my
eyes," she said. "I heard a funny kind of popping noise,
and I was there in school in class with all my friends.
It was all so clear. I could see the kids squirming and
shifting at their desks. Miss Carlyle was tugging on
the tip of her chin like she always did when she was
impatient. I could see a couple of the guys passing
notes. Then Miss Carlyle saw them, too, and made
them stand in separate corners of the room for the rest
of the class period."

That night when one of her friends called, Susan

told her about the incident.

"Cathy wanted to know how I had found out about Curly and Vernon getting caught passing notes. Of course, I didn't tell her. But I actually used this method to enable me to keep up with my classmates in school whenever I became ill."

It did not occur to the adult Susan to use this remarkable surveillance method to keep an eye on her children until about fourteen years ago, when she was thirty-three years old and suddenly hospitalized with ptomaine poisoning after eating at a small diner during a family outing.

"I lay violently ill, clenching my teeth against the terrible stomach cramps," Susan said. "I had only arrived at the emergency room an hour or so before, and I had not yet been given any medication that really alleviated my suffering."

A particularly nasty wave of nausea shuddered her body, and Susan became conscious of something she could only describe as a "wispy puff of cotton" floating away from her physical self.

"And then my consciousness was in that weird cottony puff of energy as it floated to the middle of the hospital room," she said. "There, it seemed to unravel itself into another version of me. This new body seemed to contain the 'real me,' and I could stand there and look down on my old body lying there in the bed.

"Dear God, I looked a sight. There was a tube running out of my mouth and nose, and my skin seemed the color of pale pea soup. A couple of nurses came running in and started to fuss over me.

"I suppose, at first, I thought I was dead," Susan recalled. "But I could see my physical body lying on the bed, and I was still breathing, so I thought, Aha! This is like when I was a kid home sick with a bout of chicken pox or whatever and I traveled to school in my ghost body to keep up with the kids in class."

Convinced that she now had a more complete concept of what was going on, Susan decided to move on out into the hospital corridor.

"I went on to the lounge, where I saw Al, my husband, sitting slumped in a chair smoking a cigarette. He had crossed his legs, and his left foot was jumping nervously. His hands were shaking, too, and I could see that he was really concerned about me.

"Four-year-old Bruce was sitting at a small table beside Al, coloring in the new dinosaur coloring book that I had just bought him. I wanted to yell at him when he stopped to bite off the end of the red crayon. He was always chewing the red crayons, and I was always after him to stop."

Susan's seven-year-old son, Keith, was flipping idly

through a magazine and sipping at a can of soda.

"Once again I wanted to yell!" Susan said. "Just before I had collapsed from the spoiled chicken or potato salad or whatever it was, I had already informed Keith that he had had more than his quota of soft drinks for the day."

Susan wondered where her ten-year-old daughter, Carol, was—and in the next instant she was standing beside her in the hospital gift shop.

"Bless her heart, she was looking at some get-well cards for her mommy," Susan said. "She took one down off the rack, and it was one of those kind of racy humorous contemporary cards.

"I could 'hear' Carol reading the verse. She gave a little giggle, then looked around, kind of embarrassed, to see if the clerk had seen her reading the adult verse in the card. Carol took out her little coin purse and bought me a nice flowery card."

Suddenly Susan felt herself being pulled upward. "I seemed to slip easily right through the walls. I found myself in a room where two doctors were talking about me. The older one, a rather gruff man, was wondering if they should contact the health commissioner and have him close down the diner where we had eaten."

Motherly concern—or annoyance—brought Susan's spiritual body back to Bruce, contentedly chewing on the red crayon at the very side of his father, who remained totally oblivious to his son's unauthorized snack.

"Then it was as if I was hearing a doctor speaking to a nurse at the bottom of a rain barrel," Susan said. "From some faraway place I heard him saying something about 'giving me a few more cc's,' and I felt myself being pulled away from Bruce the Crayon Chomper."

"Just like that, I was back in my physical body—and I felt terribly ill!"

When her daughter, Carol, walked in with the get-well card, Susan grimaced through her discomfort and decided that she could use a good laugh—so she repeated the naughty limerick lines that Carol had read in the contemporary card that she had put back in the rack.

"Carol got very pale, and her eyes got big and wide," Susan said. "My husband, Al, wondered if I was delirious, reciting such double-entendre doggerel in front of the kids.

"I started to bawl Brucie out for eating another red crayon, but then I stopped in midgrowl. I realized that I had discovered an incredibly potent tool that I could employ in keeping an eye on my kids."

Susan said that she decided not to disclose her out-of-body experience during her intense pain in the hospital—nor did she confess the strange talent that she had acquired when she was a youngster afflicted with a steady barrage of childhood illnesses. "I let all three of them go through their high school years believing that their mother either employed a staff of private detectives to spy on them or that she was an incredible psychic possessed of an all-seeing third eye," she said.

"It wasn't until one Christmas that I finally confessed that I had the ability to travel out of my body and that that was how I could keep such a close eye on them. Bruce was eighteen, a freshman at the university. Keith was twenty-one, halfway through his first year employed as a computer analyst. Carol was twenty-four, married, pregnant with her first child. I figured that they were all mature enough to hear the truth about their mother's unique talent.

"So I told Carol how it was that I knew exactly where she and her best friend, Melissa, were hiding on that day when the two fourteen-year-old girls decided to run away from home.

"I explained to Bruce how it was that I was able to find his bicycle when it was stolen from in front of the elementary school when he was eight.

"I carefully outlined the out-of-body procedure I employed to find the unconscious Keith on that terrible day in his junior year in high school when he suffered the hiking accident in the national park.

"In response to their individual surprise and group

skepticism, I gave them each three or four other examples of how I had been able to keep such a close watch on them.

"I don't think any of them, including my husband, Al, believed me," Susan said. "They seemed to prefer to cherish their belief that their mother was a marvelous visionary with an all-seeing third eye."

*T*here is an old Spanish proverb that says that an ounce of mother is worth a pound of clergy, so Estelle Santos was going directly to the Source when she cried out to God in an anguished prayer that awful day: "Oh, God, help us! Send us a miracle and help us lift the station wagon off Ray before he dies!"

With that heaven-sent supplication, two women and a girl sought to lift a 3,500-pound station wagon off the unconscious teenaged boy being crushed underneath its unrelenting bulk.

Ray Santos, seventeen, had been repairing the transmission of his 1978 Chevrolet in the yard of his home in Las Cruces, New Mexico, when the car slipped off a jack and pinned him.

A steel cross brace under the steering column pressed heavily, agonizingly, against his chest. The pain was unbearable. Ray tried to take a deep breath but couldn't. He realized that if he didn't get the pressure off of himself, he would be crushed to death, but every time he shouted for help, he let air out of his lungs, and the deadly weight on his chest increased. He feared that at any second, he would hear the awful sounds of his ribs cracking. The last thing he remembered before passing out was asking God to forgive his sins.

Sixty-six-year-old Felicita Madrid heard Ray's faint, frantic shouting. When she looked out of her window and saw a pair of shoes sticking out from under the station wagon, she knew that someone was dying. Mrs. Madrid's cries for help summoned Ray's mother, Estelle; their neighbor Roberta Gavarette; and Roberta's eleven-year-old daughter, Rita.

The two women and the girl grabbed hold of the station wagon's bumper, and, at the count of three, tried with all of their strength to lift it. The bumper raised up, but the wheels would not leave the ground.

Estelle prayed aloud for God's help before they tried

once again to lift the car off of Ray.

"That's when the man ran up to us," Estelle recalled. "He was not a very tall man, but he was stocky and powerfully built. His nose looked as if it had been broken. There was something about him that was fierce and wild, but his brown eyes were kind. He said that he would give us a hand.

"We figured that he was a stranger who just happened by and saw our trouble, and we were grateful for any help that we could get.

"I counted to three again; and when we lifted the bumper, the big man's muscles bulged—and the car rose completely off the ground. The station wagon now seemed no heavier than a feather." The powerful man told Felicita and Rita to pull Ray out from under the car while he and the two women held the car up above Ray's chest.

"Somehow in all the excitement of the ambulance arriving to rush Ray off to the hospital, the stranger disappeared," Estelle said. "Ray was very lucky. He was treated at a hospital, but miraculously suffered no broken bones or internal injuries. Ray was thankful to God for letting him stay around a while longer, but he was upset that we didn't get the stranger's name so he could thank him for saving his life."

That night, Felicita Madrid startled the others when she told them that she recognized the man who had appeared so fortuitously at such a desperate moment. At first, she said, she had not been certain, but after she had thought more about it, she was positive of the stranger's identity.

She explained that twenty years before, when she and her late husband, Ramon, had first moved to the neighborhood, a man named Emilio Sanchez, a powerfully built man who had wrestled professionally under the ring alias of "the Mexican Mauler," had occupied the Santoses' home. Felicita remembered vividly having watched the wrestler working out with barbells in the backyard, and she recalled the night he had been killed in an automobile accident.

"Emilio was a gentle giant," Mrs. Madrid said. "He loved people, children and young people especially, and I have often felt that I have glimpsed him in the neighborhood. He was always there to help when he was needed."

Estelle Santos summed up the feelings of everyone when she said, "God heard our prayers and spared my son Ray's life. He granted us a miracle. Who can say that God did not send us a spirit to give us a helping hand from beyond?"

$\mathcal{S}$herry Hansen Steiger has
had many experiences
that have demonstrated
the power of prayer in her life. One dramatic incident,
which involved her son, Erik, occurred in 1972.

After dinner one evening, six-year-old Erik complained
of not feeling well. At first Sherry noticed that he had only
a slight fever, but when she rechecked his temperature
about an hour later, it had escalated to 102 degrees.

An attentive mother, she was torn between attending
her weekly prayer group or staying home to minister to
her son, but her husband Paul insisted that she go to her

meeting. Since Sherry already had the kids ready for bed, he would tuck them in at the usual time, then continue to check on Erik.

Sherry agreed, then added that she would sit in the prayer circle for Erik and ask that the whole group pray for his healing. She asked that her husband "lay hands" on Erik at the preappointed time during which the group regularly focused their collective prayer. Paul confirmed the exact time with Sherry before she left for the prayer group.

The group's evening discussion became far more lively than usual. As things turned out, the "normal" time for the healing circle was quite altered by a long discussion on healing.

When the discussion finally concluded, Sherry sat in for her son. As the group began to lay hands on her, the thought struck Sherry that Paul would have followed the previously agreed-upon instructions to lay hands on Erik much earlier. Then, dismissing any anxiety over the time difference, Sherry focused on the healing energy and directed it to her son, consoling herself with the knowledge that a Greater Power than she was at work.

When Sherry arrived home, Paul, who had been asleep on the couch, sprang up with tremendous excitement to share his story. It seemed that Erik's temperature had shot up to 104 degrees while Sherry was gone. At first Paul panicked, but then he had a powerful feeling that God would heal Erik through the prayer circle. He consoled himself so thoroughly with this thought that he fell asleep on the couch.

When Paul awakened, he looked at the clock and saw that he had slept through the time when he was to lay hands on Erik, and he felt a huge pang of guilt. Erik, however, who had been sleeping beside his father, got up and began to make his way up the stairs. Startled, Paul demanded to know where Erik was going and insisted that he come back immediately to lie down.

"It's all right, Daddy," Erik told him. "Mommy's prayer healed me. I'm all better now. I'm just going to get my toys."

Paul immediately got the thermometer and took Erik's temperature. He was completely astonished to see that it was normal!

When Paul relayed his story, he included his concern about his having missed the time when he was supposed to have put his hands on Erik. He looked at his watch when Erik was on his way up the stairs after the fever had broken, and he saw that it was about an hour and a half later than the time when he was supposed to have lain hands on his son.

Miraculously, however, that was the actual time that the prayer group and Mommy had intervened on Erik's behalf.

*A*nother extraordinary demonstration of the supernatural power of prayer interceding on behalf of a child in need occurred in 1976 when Sherry and her daughter, Melissa, were living in Virginia Beach, Virginia.

Sherry had worked overtime in her advertising/public relations position in Chesapeake. After she took the baby-sitter and six-year-old Melissa to get some dinner, Sherry opened the door on the passenger side for them to get into the car.

It seemed to take a little longer than usual for the

baby-sitter to get Melissa adjusted on her lap, so Sherry walked around and got in on the driver's side, leaving the passenger door open for the baby-sitter to shut when she was comfortably situated.

As Sherry started up the car, she glanced at the baby-sitter as if to signal her to close the door. When the baby-sitter finally slammed the door shut, Melissa let out a blood-curdling scream.

Sherry pulled over to the side of the road and parked. When she looked toward Melissa to see what was wrong, she saw that her daughter's hand appeared to be smashed in the closed door!

"Open the car door! Melissa's hand is in the door!" Sherry screamed over and over, to no avail. The baby-sitter seemed unable to understand her above Melissa's cries of anguish, so Sherry got out of the car and ran around to open the door. Near panic now, she realized that her daughter's hand was completely crushed.

Racing to the nearest hospital, she arrived within minutes to the emergency entrance. The attending physician saw immediately that all of the fingers on Melissa's right hand were crushed.

While they awaited the results of the X-rays, Sherry and the baby-sitter tried to console Melissa, who was still crying in pain. At the same time, Sherry was comforting the baby-sitter, who felt completely responsible for having shut the car door before noticing that Melissa's hand was still holding on to the doorpost.

Melissa's unceasing screams pierced her mother's heart with agony, and Sherry decided to pray over her daughter's hand.

She asked the baby-sitter to join her in prayer and told her to hold one of her hands while she placed the other hand over Melissa's crushed fingers. Sherry prayed intensely out loud for God to touch and to heal her child's hand.

All of a sudden, Melissa stopped crying. Right before her very eyes, Melissa's crushed hand suddenly appeared normal—and apparently the pain had left Melissa with the instant healing.

Just then, the doctor walked in to report that the X-rays confirmed his visual diagnosis: All of Melissa's fingers were crushed.

A few moments later, he was the one who seemed in need of an attending physician when Sherry told him that Melissa was healed!

Astonished, he examined Melissa's hand and cried out, "It's a miracle! It truly is a miracle!"

*E*laine Mitsuyoshi remembered vividly the delight her mother-in-law, Rebecca, had expressed when Elaine's husband, Tom, transformed an old, rusted railroad lantern into a beautiful piece of art. His mother had purchased the lantern at a yard sale several years before, given it to her son, and forgotten all about it. Tom had retrieved it from her basement and taken it back to his own workshop to work on it.

"You have your father's talent for seeing the unusual and the lovely in the ordinary," Rebecca Mitsuyoshi had said with pride. "Who would have thought that when you found this rusty old thing in the basement you would make it into such a magnificent object of light?"

Tom had spent several evenings working on the lantern. He had sanded off the rust, restored its bright red painted surface, then wired it, and installed a bulb strategically behind the old wick. To top off his efforts, he had painted small scenes of railroad and frontier history on the base of the lamp.

"I know that I gave it to you," his mother teased, "but now that you have done such a good job on it, I think I want it back."

Tom laughed good-naturedly and gallantly offered to return it to his mother. Rebecca smiled and admitted that she was only being mischievous. "Besides," she added, "it is really too splendid to fit in with my glass turtles and ceramic animals. Let us say that it will be something to remember me by."

Tom immediately protested that he had far more wonderful things than an old lantern by which to remember his mother.

"I had a strange feeling when she made such a statement," Elaine said. "Although Mother Mitsuyoshi was in her early eighties, she was very healthy and spry. I couldn't remember her having a sick day. She still lived a very active life, and she gloried in her six children and all the activities of her twenty grandchildren. It seemed such a peculiar thing to say about the lantern."

In spite of Mrs. Mitsuyoshi's vigorous lifestyle, less than a month later, she suffered a massive stroke.

"For nearly two weeks, her indomitable spirit struggled to continue life on the earth plane," Elaine stated. "Rebecca lay in a bed in the intensive care unit of the hospital, moving back and forth over a narrow line between life and death. Tom and her other children were fearful that the stroke might leave her paralyzed or otherwise physically impaired. While they wanted their mother with them forever, they were stricken with even greater grief when they considered a scenario that would see their once active mother spending her last days as a virtual vegetable on a life-support system.

"On the fourteenth day after her stroke, the doctors told the family that Mother was doing so well that she could be transferred from the intensive care unit into a regular room and that she could begin to receive visits from her friends."

"Our prayers have been answered," Tom said on the drive home from the hospital. "We have our mother with us for a while longer, and she will soon be able to resume her normal pattern of activities."

Elaine and Tom had a quiet dinner with their two small sons, then decided to retire early for some much needed sleep.

"I was still operating on too much adrenaline to drop right off to sleep, so I decided I would read until I got drowsy enough to turn out the lights," Elaine recalled. "Because I enjoy reading in bed at night, Tom had placed the fancy refinished railroad lantern on my side of the bed. It was just the perfect height for me to read comfortably by without disturbing his slumber."

Elaine had not read for more than fifteen or twenty minutes, when she heard the two boys begin to shout and the older of their sons cry out, "Mommy, Daddy, what's that weird light doing out in the hallway?"

As she and Tom watched in astonishment, a glowing ball of orange light, about the size of a baseball and moving in a zigzag pattern, floated into their bedroom. It hovered over the two of them for a second or two, then dove for the old railroad lantern and exploded with such force that the boys heard the sound in their bedroom and came running in fear to their parents.

On a soul level of awareness, Tom knew that his mother had passed on. "Elaine," he said, his voice unsteady. "Oh, my God, I know that Mama has just been here to give us a sign that she has died."

Elaine put an arm around her husband's trembling shoulders to comfort him. She found herself speaking as if to convince herself as well as Tom. "Dear, you know that we left the hospital only a few hours ago. You know that Mother has made giant strides toward a recovery."

Tom shook his head in contradiction to her reassuring words. "Elaine, I know that Mama was just here to say goodbye. You know that the old lantern was the last thing she gave us. You remember the fuss that she made when I refinished it. Somehow, she was able to project her love so that it could connect with her last physical gift."

Tom was right. Later, the family learned that Rebecca Mitsuyoshi had slipped into a coma just a few minutes before the manifestation of the glowing ball of light in their home. She died only two hours later.

"Tom and I will always feel that his mother did visit us to say a last farewell, and that the lantern over which he had labored so lovingly had served as a catalyst to release a final burst of physical energy as she passed on."

$\mathcal{T}$he magical link between mother and child can often be puzzling to young children attempting to discern whether or not Mom really does have eyes in the back of her head!

For example, Sherry Hansen Steiger averted certain disaster one evening when she returned home from her position as counselor at the State University of New York at Stony Brook on Long Island. She had very little time to pick up her children, Melissa and Erik, and head to Smithtown Shopping Mall, where she counseled runaway teenagers and conducted a community meal program. As she entered the front door, she hurriedly yelled for her husband to get the kids into the car and that she would be there in a second.

Accustomed to going in and out of the house in such flurried departures, Sherry normally would have gone through the kitchen. But on this particular evening, in more of a hurry than usual, she went straight down the hall and out through the front door.

With the family resituated in the van and on their way down the highway, a gnawing anxiety began to build that made Sherry uneasy. After doing a physical and mental once-over check to be sure they had everything and everybody, she breathed a sigh of relief and relaxed for a few peaceful minutes, realizing everything was fine. But the closer they moved toward their destination, the more distress seemed to build. Nearly there, she suddenly blurted out, "Something is wrong. We *have* to turn around and go back home!"

At first her disturbing message fell on deaf ears. Repeating her statement in great anguish, she insisted that they turn around and go all the way back home. Obviously, since they were already running late and were only minutes from the ministries, Sherry knew it would take a very good reason to obey this command, and she didn't have anything specific—only that a gut feeling said "something is wrong back home." In fact, the feeling was so strong that she argumentatively said she would hitchhike back home if she had to, at which point her husband reluctantly and somewhat angrily turned around. The tension and nervous silence was broken only when they pulled up into the driveway of their home, and Sherry flung open the car door and flew into the house. Not having the faintest idea what she would encounter, she followed her instincts, leading her straight into the kitchen where it became obvious what she had sensed when the smell of smoke and shooting flames made it very clear that something was on fire.

Apparently Erik had pulled a kitchen chair up to the stove, turned on the burner, and put a potholder-towel over one of the burners. Not realizing the stove had been turned on, her husband had simply grabbed Erik off the chair and headed straight out to the van. Fortunately, the burner was on simmer, but that was enough to have the entire stovetop in flames shooting to the ceiling. Instinctively grabbing a pair of tongs, Sherry snatched the burning rag from the stove, tossed it into the sink, and managed to put out the rest of the fire. If the family had arrived even minutes later, the whole house would have been engulfed in flames.

Miraculously, some level of maternal awareness had alerted her to a mischievous act of her young son that could have resulted in the destruction of their home and all their belongings.

*P*arapsychologist Dr. Louisa E. Rhine's pioneering research includes numerous cases in which ESP impressions of serious or threatening circumstances were, in fact, accurate. In her *Hidden Channels of the Mind*, she tells of the experience of a woman in Wyoming who had gone to the dentist one afternoon, leaving her two-year-old daughter and her three-year-old son with a baby-sitter.

As the mother sat in the dentist's chair having a tooth filled, she suddenly felt that there was an emergency at home. "I wanted to run out of the office, but the dentist was working on my tooth," she told Dr. Rhine. "Tears began to run down my cheeks, and I became very upset."

The concerned dentist thought that he was hurting the woman or that she had become ill.

"I assured him I wasn't sick," she said, continuing her story, "but I asked him to please hurry and finish so I could get home as soon as possible."

When she reached home, the police were just bringing her little boy to the house.

"There was an ice cream man who passed our house each day," she said. "The baby-sitter had given the child some money and said that he could go and get some ice cream. Then she left the door to see about something else.

"When my little boy didn't come right back, she went to the front yard and couldn't see him anywhere. She went to the circle, looked in the fountain, and searched up and down the street."

What the baby-sitter did *not* do was call the mother at the dentist's office or her husband at work—as she had been instructed to do if anything should happen to either of the children. It was the lady next door who finally called the police.

Later, the shaken mother learned that after a woman driver had nearly struck her wandering boy on the street, she picked him up and took him to the police station.

"The policeman finally gave my son his ice cream, for he hadn't been able to catch up with the ice cream man—even though he had crossed several main streets in pursuit of him," she said. "And all this while I was at the dentist!"

*B*arry Cassidy tried his best to shut off feelings of humiliation when he considered that, at the age of thirty-six, he was once again living in his parents' home. He was in the process of obtaining a divorce so that he might marry the "other woman."

"My marriage had turned out to be a miserable facade that had crumbled around us," Barry said. "Jody and I had married right out of college, two 'yuppies' determined to get rich as fast as morally possible. I can't blame Jody for staying on the super-fast materialistic treadmill because her rewards were incredible. On the other hand, my more traditional rearing had forced me to see how shallow we were becoming, and I insisted on taking more time to smell the roses and enjoy life."

It was while walking in the park that Barry had met Morena.

"Our affair didn't shoot off with a fireworks display of passion," Barry explained. "I discovered that she jogged nearly every night in that park, and I made it a point to be there. After a few weeks, I was jogging with her back to her apartment overlooking the river."

It was during the second month that he had been living with his parents that Barry's mother suffered a massive stroke.

"I hoped that my personal problems had not prompted Mom's stroke," Barry recalled. "Dad assured me that their doctor had tried to warn her to take it easier and that it was, sadly, perhaps in the order of natural events.

"I was coming home from seeing Morena at about 1:30 in the morning when I saw nearly every light in the house shining out at me. Because Mom had been in intensive care for four days, I got a really queasy feeling in the pit of my stomach."

Barry found his father, Dick, and his sister, Lori, sitting at the dining room table silently sipping coffee.

"As soon as they looked up at me, I knew that Mom was dead. Lori's eyes were swollen from crying, and Dad looked pale and drawn. He looked far older than his sixty-two years when he told me that Mom had died of a massive coronary just a few hours before."

Lori left for her apartment around 2:30, and Barry's father went into his bedroom to lie down and attempt to get some rest.

"I decided to sit in the old recliner in the living room before going to bed. Because of the light coming from the chandelier in the dining room, I could have read if I had wished, but I chose to lean back and permit the memories of Mom to come forth unchecked.

"I remembered how frightened I was to leave her side and to start my first day at school. I would never forget the kind manner in which she comforted me when my best friend, Grandpa Martin, had died. My brain was flooded with images of bruised knees, teeth under my pillow for the tooth fairy, and the best oatmeal cookies in the world. Then I thought of the dream that she had related just a few weeks after I had moved back home."

Barry had been astonished when his mother, Lorna Cassidy, had told him that she had dreamed of her own death. "Buddy," she had begun, calling him by her pet name for him, "I saw myself walking toward beautiful green, rolling meadows with the loveliest flowers imaginable. I was wearing a white, flowing robe, and I was following a path that I knew would lead me to heaven."

Barry felt the tears coming as he spoke aloud to the empty room, "Oh, Mom, did you know that you were going to die? Did you know that your time to move on to a higher dimension was almost upon you?"

"*Yes!*" a voice cried.

The voice that answered Barry made his spine go rigid. Startled, he searched the room for whoever had answered his unspoken question.

"It was a woman's voice," Barry remembered, "that I knew for certain. And I also knew that the voice sounded exactly like my mother's."

Barry nervously decided that he had fallen asleep in the comfortable recliner and had dreamed of his mother. It was time, he argued convincingly, to go to bed and try to fall back to sleep.

"That's when I saw Mom. She appeared as a transparent figure, glowing with a soft, white light. She said that she had come back to warn me, but first she wanted to tell me that she had been walking on those same green, rolling meadows that she had seen in her dream."

She went on to say that there was no pain or hatred where she was now, only peace and contentment.

"And if you want some peace and contentment in your earth life," she warned Barry, "you had better listen to what I have to say! Morena is not the kind of woman that you now believe her to be. If you go ahead and divorce Jody to marry Morena, you will be sorry. Your future will not be at all as you now imagine it. You believe that Morena is giving you another chance at happiness. I tell you, my son, that you are, instead, taking a chance with your immortal soul! If you should not heed my advice, Barry, and if you should marry Morena, she will divorce you within three years of your marriage. And she will be merciless in the settlement!"

Barry said that his mother's spirit form stayed with him for about five minutes. "I kept pinching myself and touching my eyes to be certain that I was awake and not dreaming. Then, because I was so very much in love with Morena, I began to question Mom about the validity of her warning. Surely, she must be mistaken."

The spirit form remained adamant. "My son, that woman is not as you believe her to be. She will hurt you terribly if you marry her."

To his everlasting regret, Barry managed to convince himself that his mother's spirit visit had been only a troubled dream brought about by his grief and distress.

"If only I hadn't been such a rationalist, such a materialist," Barry says today. "If only I hadn't believed myself to be so much in love with Morena. Mom's advice from the spirit world proved to be totally accurate. Morena brought me to new depths of despair when we divorced after three years of a miserable marriage."

$\mathcal{A}$s one of the founding members of the Holistic Healing Board through the Institutes of Health and Welfare in Washington, D.C., in 1978, Sherry Hansen Steiger learned of a research project that revealed yet another invisible link between mother and child. Newborn infants in the nursery and their respective mothers in their various hospital rooms were monitored for both audible sounds and internal responses by special sensing devices. Even though the nursery and the mothers' rooms were placed far apart—and the mothers' rooms had been soundproofed as an additional condition of the test—it was noted that whenever an infant would begin to cry, its own mother's breasts would begin to fill with milk even though the mother was unable to hear the child with her "physical" ears. An invisible two-way connection seems to exist between mother and child that tells the mother when her child is hungry or in distress. ◯

*O*n many occasions, some invisible sense of danger looming over her children has prompted Sherry to take the necessary action to save their lives.

While on a vacation to Florida back in 1972, Sherry; her husband, Paul; their two children, Erik and Melissa; and two teenaged friends, Jan and Jimmy, escaped terrible death by heeding the warning that was transmitted to them through Sherry's special "radar."

Driving straight through to Florida from Columbus, Ohio, in an oversized van that had been customized for sleeping and storing camp gear, the group arrived at their campsite tired, yet enthusiastic enough to set up the tents that night. For the next two days, they enjoyed beach walks, building sandcastles, collecting shells, and burying each other in the sand.

On the third night at the campsite, all parties were tucked into their sleeping bags and had been sound asleep for many hours when all of a sudden, Sherry sat up in her sleeping bag and screamed, "We've got to get out of here—now!"

Nearly in a trance state, Sherry repeated these instructions until all were awake. By this time, her family had learned not to question her instincts, as there had been sufficient experiences to prove them valid.

On this occasion, however, Paul had an edge to his voice when he asked, "I don't understand. Why do we have to leave now? The sky is clear; all the stars are brightly shining; all else in the campground is completely quiet. What could possibly be wrong?"

Somewhat puzzled herself, Sherry answered, "I honestly have no idea. I just *know* that if we don't leave now something terrible is going to happen to our children."

Jan and Jimmy already had Erik and Melissa in their arms and were awaiting instructions outside the tent. When Sherry went out and saw the clear night air and observed the extreme quiet and peace that seemed to be all around the campground area, she acknowledged that she, too, felt it was weird to ask everyone to leave. But she also knew that it was *necessary*.

Coming up with where to go and what to do was the next item of business. Sherry thought of an idea that must have sounded insane at four o'clock in the morning—taking all their dirty laundry to the next town to a Laundromat. Then at least they would be doing something constructive during their getaway.

It took about forty-five minutes to arrive at the next town. They had monitored the radio for a message alerting them to a storm or some such danger, but there was no indication of any sort of omen or portent of disaster. What could they do but make the best of it? They all sang songs until they reached the Laundromat, then everyone pitched in to do the many loads of wash.

Finding an open convenience store for change for the washing machines and dryers offered them an opportunity to ask the clerk if he had heard of a storm moving in, a monster lurking in a nearby campground— anything! But once again, all seemed to be peaceful and quiet.

By now the first hues of dawn were coloring the sky, and with clean, dry, fresh-smelling towels and beach clothes (and clean diapers for one-year-old Melissa), the group loaded up the van and turned to Sherry for the sign to return to camp.

Singing all the way back to the campground, they had all but forgotten the reason they had left—until they couldn't find their tents.

Driving into the campground, all they could see was a vacant lot where their camp had been set up. Scattered cans from the food boxes and clothes were tossed here and there, as if some incredible force had thrown them about.

The family got out of the van and stood looking at the scene in a complete daze.

Just then, a park ranger drove up and excitedly bolted out of his truck. "Oh, my God! Thank heavens you are all safe," he said. "We have been conducting a search for your family. We thought you all must have been killed!

"We have just had the most incredible freak occurrence of nature I've ever seen in my over thirty-five years as a park ranger. Somewhere around 4:30 A.M. or so, maybe a tad later, out of nowhere—and I mean *nowhere*—came this waterspout from the ocean—out of a clear sky!

"It swept onto the campground with no warning and with no time for anyone to act or to warn others. It tossed your tents in the air like they were kites. It picked them up, spun them around, and tossed them in all different directions. We are still finding things from your camp area scattered everywhere!"

The park ranger explained that a waterspout is like a "mini-tornado" or small hurricane that comes in off the ocean with incredible force and then either dissipates or goes back out to sea. He suddenly looked Sherry square in the eyes and asked, "Excuse my language, but how in the hell did you get the kids and all out in time? What happened? Where did you go at this time of the morning? You can't believe how worried we have been," he continued. "There is no conceivable way that you would have escaped unhurt. More than likely, if you had all been asleep in your tents—as we assumed you were—you would have all been in pieces around the area with the rest of your belongings. You really must have angels surrounding you guys!"

After Sherry explained her sudden feeling that the lives of her children were endangered, the ranger simply looked at them and shook his head, saying, "Boy, this is sure one for the books! Come, let me show you where your tents ended up."

They followed the ranger to view the twisted, mangled tents with the stakes piercing the fabric at various points.

Sherry and her family stood in awe. After taking a few pictures of the carnage as a lasting reminder of their narrow escape, they all shed tears and offered many prayers of thanks that their lives had been spared.

On an earlier occasion when her daughter was an infant, Sherry's seemingly supernatural knowledge of an accident that was about to occur may have saved the life of her baby and the rest of her family as well. Sherry; her husband, Paul; and their two small children, Erik and Melissa, were on their way to their evening ministry at Smith Haven Mall on Long Island. Sherry was nursing Melissa in the front passenger seat of the car while Paul drove. Erik was busy playing with his toy cars in the backseat.

Sherry's attention was entirely on Melissa. She valued this bonding time and offset the jiggling of the car, the traffic noise, and the rush to their place of employment with extra loving as she calmly stroked her daughter's arm and back.

Suddenly Sherry was struck with an awful feeling that something was about to harm her three-month-old nursing at her breast. At the same time, she received guidance as to how to protect her baby. Having absolutely no idea what the imminent threat might be and without removing her fixed gaze from Melissa for even a split second, Sherry screamed out as firmly and loudly as possible without shattering her daughter's eardrums, "Paul, steer hard to the right now! *Now ... to the right ... now!*"

She must have uttered the words with enough force and conviction to cause Paul not to question her, but to simply act immediately on the shouted order.

In that indescribable moment that seemed to last an eternity, Sherry was dimly aware of the crashing and bending of metal, the squealing of brakes, the breaking of glass—all spinning around in her head as if they were each part of a dream.

When their Ford Mustang finally came to a stop, it became apparent that Sherry and her family had just been involved in a major automobile accident. In a grateful stupor they looked at each other, offering a silent prayer of thanks that not one of them was injured.

From the rear left side, a drunk driver had gunned his truck out of a bar's parking lot and roared into the street, heading straight for the driver's door of the Mustang at a speed of about sixty-five miles an hour. Even if Sherry had been looking at the road instead of at Melissa, it would have been impossible from her point of view to see the truck approaching. Somehow that mysterious motherly protective instinct that transcends time, space, and the physical senses miraculously saved not only her two children but herself and her husband as well. Because Paul had acted, without the slightest hesitation, turning the steering wheel hard to the right, the truck had become severely entangled in the right rear of the Mustang, just behind the back door. Erik, who fortunately had been on the other side of the backseat, was the most miraculously spared.

When the police arrived, they were baffled as to how the family had escaped serious injury. Several witnesses described how the truck seemed almost to target the car, how it appeared to speed right toward the Mustang.

The police had trouble seeing how Paul could have steered fast enough and hard enough to escape a more direct hit from the charging truck. And how, the officers asked, did Paul know to steer to the right? If the larger vehicle had hit the driver's door of the Mustang, the police officers said, Paul, Sherry, and Melissa would more than likely have been killed, considering the speed and force with which the truck would have struck them.

Sherry was too busy comforting her little ones to explain, so Paul, shaken as he was, described the chain of events to the officers.

All they could say by way of intelligent response was, "That must be some motherly love. We'd say you had a few angels watching over you, too!"

There is no doubt that both of those aspects of divine energy had interceded on the family's behalf, for it took police officers and a fire department rescue squad more than three hours to pry the two vehicles apart. ✆

*L*eah Fellenstein of Highland Park, Illinois, has a clear memory of the morning in March 1953 when her mother, Rhonda Demske, received a strong telepathic message that Leah's grandmother, Sarah Lebowitz, had passed away.

"We lived at the time in Columbus, Ohio, and Gram and Grandpa Lebowitz resided in East Brunswick, New Jersey," Leah said. "I was not quite eight. My sister, Maxine, was five. I remember clearly that I was setting the table for breakfast when Mom came down the stairs crying and saying, 'Gram passed away during the night.'"

Leah nearly dropped the plates that she was carrying to the table, and little Maxine, perceiving their mother in tears, began to sob in concert.

"Her head lowered and her hands cupped over her eyes, Mom walked slowly toward the large easy chair in the living room and sat down," Leah said. "I ran to her side to comfort her. Even at that young age, I knew that my mother and her mom were extremely close."

It was at that moment that Leah's father, George Demske, entered the living room. He still had shaving cream specks on his chin and beneath his ears. It was obvious that he had heard the sounds of his wife weeping and had come to see what the matter was.

"Rhonda," he wanted to know, "what's wrong? Have you a stomachache?"

As his wife divulged the reason for her great sorrow, George Demske's expression altered from one of commiseration to one of incredulity.

"How is it that you know this, darling?" he asked in a gentle voice. "There has been no telegram delivered. We have received no long-distance telephone calls. We have received no message of any kind that would bring us such terrible news."

Eight-year-old Leah put her arms around her younger sister and began to relax. "I began to think that maybe Mom had only dreamed about Gram's death," she said. "Papa was always calm and collected. If he said that there had been no telephone calls or telegrams to inform us of Gram's death, then that meant that she was still alive."

But her mother was firm in her grief. "You know that Mama and I have our own private telephone line," she reminded her family. "We have always known things about each other without speaking."

There was no question that Gram and Mom seemed always to be in touch on some level of awareness. Leah and Maxine had wondered if they might be witches or something.

George knelt to take his wife's hands tenderly in his own, his thick fingers ink-stained from the printing presses that he operated for the newspaper. He readily conceded the special bond that Rhonda had with her mother, but he wished to make a point of his own.

"Perhaps this time you have only had a vivid dream," he said. "You know that your mother is well and that she enjoys perfect health. It was only three months ago at Hanukkah that we saw both of your parents. It has been less than a week since you spoke to her on the telephone. It is a blessing that she is so well."

Leah nodded her head in silent agreement with her father's analysis of the situation. Gram always presented a picture of glowing vitality.

Gram herself often boasted to Leah and Maxine that she had needed a doctor only twice in her life—once to give birth to their mother and once to give birth to Uncle Ira. Leah knew that her mother had been born when Gram was very young. Even now, it seemed as though they might be sisters, rather than mother and daughter.

Rhonda Demske dabbed at her large brown eyes with a handkerchief and spoke to her family in a hushed but firm voice: "Gram . . . my mother . . . died last night. I *know* that she did."

"I went back to setting the table," Leah said. "I didn't know what else to do. Mom gave a deep sigh, whispered something to Daddy about life going on, and said that she would make breakfast. But before she could begin, a telegram arrived from Uncle Ira saying that Gram had died suddenly and quite unexpectedly during the night. She had suffered a heart attack.

"With that sad confirmation of Mom's *knowing,* none of us felt like eating that morning. Papa held Mom in his arms, and Maxine and I hugged her legs and cried."

Forty-four years later, Leah Fellenstein vividly recalled the details of that morning in March 1953. Her mother's accurate *knowing* of Grandmother Lebowitz's death would transform the rest of Leah's life.

"Mom had no clue that Gram was ill. Gram was only forty-five years old, and she had been healthy and robust when we had seen her three months before at Hanukkah. Mom had spoken to her on the telephone only five nights before her death. Gram herself had no clue that she was on the verge of a heart attack.

"At the age of eight, I was given profound proof of the spiritual level of communication that exists between all humans—and perhaps reaches its most complete expression between a mother and her child," Leah said. "I did not hesitate to work together with my own children, Daniel and Ruth, to create a strong love connection and to develop our own psychic connection as well. We have often been able to use this bond to great advantage throughout the many stages of our mother-child relationship."

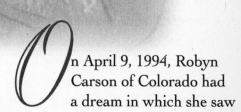

On April 9, 1994, Robyn Carson of Colorado had a dream in which she saw her mother, Donna Jacobson, lying on her side on the street in a pool of blood.

"I woke up in a cold sweat," Robyn said. "I always had a close connection with my mother, and we had experienced many telepathic exchanges ever since my early childhood. Four years before, Mom had dreamed of Dad's fatal heart attack while he was away on business, and now I had had a dream about her death that was so vivid that I began to worry. I telephoned her at once, even though it was only seven o'clock in the morning and I knew that Mom usually slept until around nine."

Robyn had intended to tell her mother about the terrible nightmare so they might interpret it together. But her mother's remarkable opening words chilled her heart: "Oh, Robyn, I am so glad you called. I've been awake for hours, unable to go back to sleep. I had an awful dream last night. My car was hit by a big truck— and I was killed! Oh, Robyn, I saw myself lying in the street in a pool of blood. It all seemed so real!"

Robyn was nearly struck speechless by her mother's revelation that they had experienced a dual dream of death. She resolved not to mention her own dream and to remain calm and reassuring for her mother's sake.

"If anything happens to me, dear, I want you to have my collection of antique plates," her mother said. "Your brother may have the wildlife paintings that he loves so much. You may divide your father's athletic trophies."

"Nothing is going to happen to you, Mom," Robyn said. "You just had a bad dream. Remember, that book on dream interpretation you found in the library said that when you dream of your death, it is very often a symbol of change coming in your life."

Her mother sighed and said that she had already thought of that. "This dream was very different from any dream that I have ever had. It was so real. I think that I have actually dreamed about my death."

Donna Jacobson talked more about how the large truck ran a red light at an intersection and crashed broadside into her car. "As if I were some rag doll, I was tossed out of my car and onto the street," she told her daughter. "It was so awful to see myself lying there with that pool of blood getting larger and larger."

Robyn continued to provide optional symbolic interpretations for the horrible images of death that her mother's dreaming mind had so vividly dramatized.

"I finally managed to change the subject to my brother Jim's approaching September wedding, one of Mom's favorite topics, but the diversion was short-lived," she said. "Mom began to worry that she might not be alive to see her only son married at last at the age of thirty-five."

That night, Robyn Carson had another dream. She was seated among a large number of friends and relatives at some kind of party or formal gathering. Food and drink were being passed on trays, but the occasion for the party seemed a somber one. On one level of awareness, she knew that she was attending a funeral and that it was quite likely her mother's.

"Certain of my friends and relatives kept coming up to me and asking if I had met a Mr. Wellington," she said. "When I would say that I had not had the pleasure, they would step aside as if to introduce me to the man. Strangely, though, I could never see his face. And when I would extend my hand in greeting, he would always seem to disappear."

Then, Robyn recalled that Carlyn Leuthauser, her high school math teacher, had suddenly appeared in the dream and asked her to remember a sequence of numbers.

"Although Mrs. Leuthauser had been dead for twelve years or more, in the alternate reality of my dream she was as hard-nosed a taskmaster as always," Robyn said. "Mrs. Leuthauser told me that I would be tested very soon and that it was important that I remember the correct order of the numbers. At first I had difficulty hearing the numbers, and I asked her several times to repeat the sequence. At last she walked away from me smiling in triumph when I successfully repeated the correct order of the digits, and she reminded me that a test would be coming soon."

The next morning at 8:15 A.M., as Robyn Carson was preparing to leave for work, the neighbor's dog began a peculiar howling that upset her in a way that she could not understand. "It was as if that mournful sound were touching me deep inside."

A few minutes later, at about 8:20, when the friends with whom she carpooled arrived to pick her up, Robyn began to weep uncontrollably as she got into the car. "My friends were immediately concerned," she said. "I felt so very embarrassed, but I didn't know what was wrong with me. I told them that I would be fine in a few minutes, and I shrugged off their suggestions that I had been working too hard. By the time they dropped me off at work at 8:53, I had managed to stop crying, but I still had an awful sense of foreboding."

Within the hour, Robyn Carson's brother, Jim, telephoned her at work with the sad news that their mother had been killed at around 8:22 that morning.

"She had had an early appointment that morning with her beautician," Robyn explained. "A massive trailer truck was unable to stop for the red light, and it skidded through the intersection and hit Mom's car while still moving at a high speed. Mom was thrown from the car and was found lying on her right side in a pool of blood.

"Her death, we were told, had been instantaneous and it had occurred at the very minute that I had suddenly begun to cry in front of my friends in the car pool.

"As an eerie addendum to the tragically accurate dreams of my mother's impending death, the name of the truck driver, who escaped injury, was Richard *Wellington*. The license number of his truck comprised the same series of numerals that my old schoolteacher in my dream had admonished me to remember."

*M*ichael Finnegan of Camden, New Jersey, says that he will swear to his dying day that his amazing experience was a true event and not merely a dream. When Finnegan was only five years old, he was lying in a hospital bed, recovering from a tonsillectomy. He had just regained consciousness, and he remembers that the ward was completely dark except for one little light down the corridor.

"I lay there trying to understand where I was," Finnegan said. "I figured out that the light was probably coming from a nurse's desk lamp, and I wished that there could be more light around me so that I could better see the strange hospital environment."

A few moments later he heard a voice whisper, "Michael, your mother is here to see you."

Overjoyed that his mother had somehow managed to stay at the hospital to await his return to consciousness, Finnegan looked up and saw a woman standing by the foot of his bed.

"She was dressed in street clothes and wore a coat that I had never before seen on my mother," he recalled. "Then when I looked at her face, I realized that I had never seen the woman before in my life. She was a total stranger to me. I thought that there had been some kind of mix-up. She was some other boy's mother, not mine.

"My throat felt too sore to ask who she was, but before I could make any sound at all, she disappeared. I lay in my bed quite disturbed, believing that I had seen a ghost, for I knew that I was not asleep and that I was not dreaming."

Finnegan said that years later, the woman he knew as his mother confessed that she was actually his stepmother. She had married his father when Michael was but an infant, and they had decided it would be better that the boy grow up believing that she was his biological mother.

"My real mother had been killed in an automobile

accident only a few months after my birth," Finnegan said. "When my stepmother showed me some photographs of my real mother, I could hardly believe my eyes. The woman in the pictures and the woman who had appeared and disappeared at my hospital bed were one and the same."

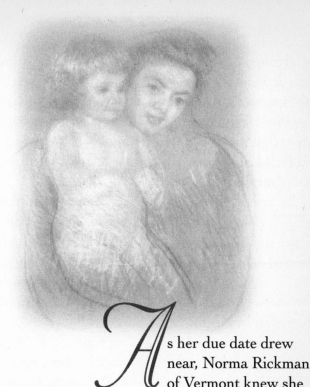

*A*s her due date drew near, Norma Rickman of Vermont knew she would have a difficult delivery. The doctors had debated whether or not they should take the child through Caesarean section, but decided to try to manipulate the breech baby in the delivery room.

Because she would have to help, Norma would be given only a mild painkiller.

"Then, the worst happened," Norma said. "My obstetrician, Dr. Millard, was out of town when the labor pains began. The pediatrician with whom

Dr. Millard had discussed my case had broken both legs
in an automobile accident two days before I went to
the hospital. Unfortunately, the doctor who finally got
corralled into delivering my baby was hardly the best
example the medical field could offer. He seemed barely
interested in the difficulty of the delivery or in alleviating
any of my pain."

As her dilation neared completion, the birthing
agonies were nearly driving Norma out of her mind.
"I was thirty-four years old. This was my first child,
my first delivery, and I felt that I was losing my sanity,"
Norma remembered. "Then, I felt a strange whirling
sensation, like I was a propeller on an airplane. My body
seemed to spin faster and faster—and then, pop! I was
floating over the bed in the labor room, looking down on
my physical body and the solicitous nurse who sought to
ease my pain."

Norma recalled that she was shocked to see how
contorted her facial features were. "At first I thought
that I had died in childbirth," she said. "My mother and
sister had been worried that I was too old to endure a
breech birth for my very first delivery. I had worried
that they might be right. And now it appeared as though
they were correct, and I had died.

"But then the body on the bed below me thrashed
wildly and let out a terrible cry of pain. I was really

baffled. That *was* me down on the bed writhing in what was obviously awful agony. But it was *also* me up near the ceiling, watching the scene below and feeling absolutely no pain at all!

"Then I seemed to be somewhere far away in the clouds . . . or heaven . . . or somewhere out in space."

Norma was astonished to see a lovely young woman with long blond hair and unusually large blue eyes smiling at her. She was dressed in a red-and-white pinafore outfit that suggested a clothing style worn by women in the latter part of the nineteenth century.

"I wondered if she was an angel," Norma said, "but she looked more like a frontier or country woman than an angel."

The young blond woman had a truly beautiful smile, and her words of sympathy were uttered in a strangely jocular manner. "I'm sorry that you're having such a difficult time, my dear. But, remember, it was your choice. You wanted to be the mother this time."

Norma wanted to ask the woman what she meant, but she was becoming conscious of a tugging, a pulling sensation.

"You'd better get on with it," the attractive blond woman told her. "It's nearly over. You'd better go back. The child is about to make its appearance."

Norma seemed to be dragged into some kind of

tunnel with a bright light at the end.

"For the first time in what seemed like days, I thought of my poor husband, Max, sitting in the waiting room," Norma said. "Just like that, I was hovering over him, watching him play a nervous game of solitaire in the visitors' lounge. My mother was also there, trying to stay calm by knitting booties for her unborn grandchild.

"The next thing I knew, I was opening my eyes and a nurse was bending over me with my baby in her hands. 'It's a girl!' she said as she gave her to me. 'A healthy baby girl!'"

Norma felt a warm surge of mother love as she accepted the wonderful prize of her daughter from the smiling nurse. It had been a long and difficult pregnancy and an extremely painful delivery. She truly did feel as though she were being presented with an award for courage befitting a good mother. She knew that she would value her child that much more for having paid such a high price in sweat, blood, tears, and agony.

"We're calling her Julia," Norma announced to the attentive nurse and to the world at large. Even the disinterested doctor nodded his silent approval.

"It would have been Throckmorton if it had been a boy," she added facetiously, testing the remote possibility that anyone in the delivery room would be interested.

"Hey," the nurse asked her, "where did you go? You

left us there for a while, didn't you?"

Norma nodded. "I did. But I surely don't know where I went. No place on this planet, that's for sure."

In the excitement and challenge of motherhood rather late in life, Norma put the strange out-of-body projection during Julia's birth completely out of her mind. And in the ensuing years, she found more than enough tasks to divert her attention from that peculiar incident as she sought to balance her career as a corporate attorney with her responsibility as a mother.

It wasn't until Julia was eight years old that the unusual experience of her birth suddenly came into focus for her mother once again.

The child had developed a rather high fever, and Norma had maintained a vigil at her bedside long into the night, placing cool washcloths on Julia's forehead and brushing aside the damp strands of her long blond hair.

About three in the morning, just before the fever broke, Julia began to whimper and toss fitfully in her sleep. A few minutes later, she awoke with a start and sat up, her large blue eyes suddenly wide open.

"Here, honey," Norma said, gently bringing a glass to her daughter's lips, "take a couple of sips of water. Your fever has broken. You're going to feel better now."

Julia dutifully took small swallows of water from the drinking glass, then reached up to hug her mother. "Oh,

Mommy," she said. "I was having that funny dream again."

Norma wanted to know what dream that might be.

"The one where you and I are all alone in the room with the bright light," Julia answered. "Where was that funny room, Mommy?"

Although Norma had first assumed that Julia had simply experienced a bizarre dream inspired by her fever, the child persisted in her desire to have the location of the "funny room with the bright light" identified.

After a series of questions—all met and negated by Julia's serious replies—Norma was about to conclude that the child's fever had somehow triggered a memory of the delivery room at the hospital at the time of her birth. There had been some medical research, Norma was aware, that suggested that some people did possess actual memories of their birth experience.

"No, no, it wasn't the delivery room, Mommy." Julia's response was once again firm. "It was before that. Before I was born."

Norma laughed aloud. "What do you mean 'before that'? There is no 'before' birth in a delivery room."

Julia sat up with an impatient frown and placed her hands on her hips for emphasis. "Yes, there is! We were in that bright room trying to decide who was going to be

the mother this time. You said that you wanted to be—
and I said, 'All right. If you want to be.' Now, *where* was
that room, Mommy? I keep trying to remember."

Norma looked at Julia—the stubborn, determined
set to her chin, her long blond hair, her blue eyes
narrowed intently—and suddenly she remembered that
strange out-of-body projection during the trauma of
childbirth.

"For a weird moment there," she said, "I was seeing
the beautiful, blue-eyed blond woman in the red-and-
white pinafore dress expressing sympathy for my
discomfort—but reminding me with a slight haughtiness
that it was my choice to be the mother this time.

"I had never told anyone about the strange
experience that had occurred during Julia's birth—not
even my husband or my mother or my sister. I had
simply attributed the whole thing to a weird hallu-
cination brought on by the intense pain of birthing a
first child—and a breech birth at that.

"I had never really thought much about the
possibility of past lives or reincarnation," Norma said.

"I know that my great love for Julia began long
before her actual physical birth, but I had always
believed that I had bonded so strongly with her because
of the severe discomfort that I suffered during my
pregnancy and the delivery.

"Who knows? Maybe it is possible that our love connection goes back *long* before her physical birth this time around. Maybe it goes back even long before the two of us sat in the room with the bright light where we decided who would be the mother this time around."

*I*n 1947, when Joel Devers of Glendale, Arizona, was eleven years old and lived with his parents in Queens, New York, he suffered a severe attack of bronchial asthma late one afternoon in January. Before his mother could summon a doctor, Joel felt himself slipping into unconsciousness.

"All at once I felt peaceful and completely relaxed," he said. "The *real* part of me just seemed to float above that poor wheezing kid on the bed, and it didn't seem to bother me at all that the physical me couldn't breathe. I had never before—or since—experienced such a wonderful sense of freedom. I had a sense that I was dying—or at least the physical me was dying—but I was remarkably untroubled by that awareness."

Joel said that he later learned that he had been in a kind of coma for nearly forty-five minutes, but he seemed totally free of the confines of time and space. "I can remember that I just seemed to hang around my room, kind of floating here and there. I don't remember seeing any angels or the white light that I have since heard other people mentioning."

He has a vivid memory of seeing the doctor come puffing into his bedroom. "Oh, no," the real me thought. "Now he's going to do something to make me breathe again, and I'll have to go back to that scrawny, sickly, wheezing body!"

The doctor shot a powerful jolt of Adrenalin into Joel's unconscious body, but the lad tried his best to resist being pulled back into the lump of clay that was so susceptible to disease and physical ailments.

"I really didn't want to go back," Joel said. "I mean, I was what today's kids call a nerd. I was a skinny, sickly, bespectacled bookworm with chronic asthma, always coming down with one illness after another. I really felt that I was much better off being a ghost or spirit or whatever I was in that state. And I truly felt that it was my decision whether to go back to my physical body or to remain in that realm of nonphysical being."

Then Joel became aware of his mother praying at his bedside. "Right there in front of the doctor, Mom started praying out loud for my life to be spared, for me to come back to them. Then she started to cry. Dad had come home from work, and when he entered my room and heard my mother's prayers, tears ran down his cheeks.

"I really felt torn by a moment of decision. Mom was telling God how much I meant to her and Dad, how much meaning I gave to their lives. I was really touched to hear her prayer. I guess I had always felt that they were as disgusted with my illnesses as I was."

Joel stopped struggling and allowed himself to be pulled back into his body. "I opened my eyes, took a deep, shuddering kind of breath, and was at once conscious of terrible pain in my chest and back."

Joel recovered from the severe attack, but he continued to suffer from his asthmatic condition.

When he was twelve, his sister Naomi was born and when it appeared that she, too, was asthmatic, Joel's parents made the decision to move to Arizona where the dry desert air was recommended for their children's health.

"I have learned to value my time here on this physical plane," Joel said. "My health improved almost at once after our move to the Phoenix area. I'm now in my sixties with grandchildren. Life has been good to me, and although I have never forgotten the near-death experience that showed me that to die is to enter a free, spiritual state—neither have I forgotten the power that lay in my mother's prayer for me to be brought back to life."

*M*y mother passed away on September 8, 2000. She told me the day before she died that she was ready to go. Unfortunately, I didn't know that she meant the very next day. I still feel really bad about that.

I lived in San Jose, California, but I had moved in with Mom, who lived in Gilroy, 30 miles away, to take care of her because she was very sick with bone cancer and her doctor had given her three to six months to live. The Hospice of the Valley that was assigned to her by her doctor was wonderful. They gave her free medication for her pain; they had someone come in three times a week to bathe her; and a nurse came twice a week to check on her.

Mom lasted only a month after the doctor diagnosed her. It seemed that she decided when she was going to leave this world, and she chose to die from a stroke, not the bone cancer.

The Sunday after she passed away, I felt a very deep urge to go to church. Even though I was raised Roman Catholic, I never went to church, not even with Mom when she was alive. But I woke up that Sunday knowing that I just had to go. My thoughts were very much on my mom. She had passed away only three days before, so I was feeling very sad.

As I set out that Sunday with my cousin, I felt a very strong pull to attend a specific Catholic church. Somehow, I felt my mom really wanted me to be there. During the mass, I discovered that it was a special observance for people who had passed away that month. I began thinking about my mother and when the priest began reading the names of the people who had recently died, I was thinking maybe I should have let him know about Mom.

And then I heard him say Mom's name.

I was very surprised that Mom's name was mentioned, and I was so pleased that she was remembered at that special mass, but I wondered how the priest could even have known her. Mom was a very sweet, shy person who didn't have any friends in Gilroy. Most of her friends and family lived in Texas.

I had called the church the week before Mom died and asked for a priest to come and pray for her, but one never showed up. I know that the priest officiating at the mass had never met my mother, and she was not a member of that church. In fact, she had never attended that church.

All I know for certain is that it was the spirit of my mother who urged me to go to church that day and to attend that particular church so that I could be there when her name was called out. I'm so glad that I *listened* and followed my instincts.

The Hospice of the Valley, which had been thoughtful in their assistance to my mother, gave me bereavement counseling after her passing. I am now a volunteer for them, so I can repay them for all their wonderful services. ☙

—GLORIA TORRES

*A*my Hargis of Bakersfield, California, awakened about 11:30 one May evening in 1978 with a terrible case of indigestion as a result of having eaten too much unripe fruit. She described the pain as "absolutely unbearable."

"Even though we had strict parental orders to the contrary, my kid brother, Billy, and I never could resist munching on the green apples from the trees in our yard," Amy said. "He was spending the night with a friend, and I was glad that he wasn't home to squeal on me. With his cast-iron stomach, I doubted if he even had gas pains—and there was no way that I was going to tell our folks that I had once again gorged myself on green apples.

"But then Mom's diagnosis of my symptoms convinced her that I was having an appendicitis attack, and she called our family doctor, Dr. Samuel Pergande. Because he was a close friend of my father's, he said he would come over and see what was wrong with me."

As Amy lay thrashing about in agony, her thoughts began to fixate on the possibility of being somehow able to escape the pain that had seemed to fill every corner of her being. How wonderful it would be to leave her pain-wracked body and just fly off and go somewhere else until the agony was over.

A spasm of pain doubled her over, and the sudden movement seemed to shoot "the thinking part" of her up to the ceiling.

"I could actually see Mom fussing about, and I could see me—that is, my physical body—tossing about on the bed, whimpering and crying," Amy said. "But the *real me* couldn't feel a thing. Miraculously, the pain somehow stayed down on the bed with my physical body. I remember feeling kind of ashamed and embarrassed about the way the physical me was behaving like such a baby. I decided that I really should go back and be grown-up about my stomachache.

"Just like that, I was back inside my body, howling and tossing about in pain. It really hurt in my body, and since there was absolutely no pain when I was outside of my body, it didn't take me long to decide where I wanted to be. I doubled over and moaned like I did before—though I really don't know if that had anything to do with it—and I was back up floating on the ceiling."

It wasn't long before Amy discovered that while she was in this altered state of consciousness she was completely free of the normal physical restrictions of time and space.

"I wondered when Doctor Sam was going to arrive, and I was suddenly inside his car as he stopped at a traffic light," Amy said. "'Why the hell do they keep these darn things going all night?' he was mumbling. 'Why don't they just keep them flashing on yellow?'"

Amy rode along with the doctor for a while; then she thought about her mother and about her physical body back in her bedroom.

"This time when I shot back to my room, my body was lying very still—and Mom was crying. I could see why. I looked terrible. My face was kind of a greenish gray, and my mouth was hanging open."

It was at that moment that Amy was startled to hear her mother begin to pray to God to spare the life of her only daughter.

"I had never thought of Mom as the spiritual, praying type," Amy said. "But I remembered Mom talking about how she had grown up in this little town in Iowa where they went to church twice every Sunday. She surely had not forgotten how to pray. She really impressed me with her eloquence. God would have to be listening to this prayer and He would have to be really impressed, too."

By this time, Amy's father, William Bucknell, had at last been roused from his sleep by the apparent seriousness of his daughter's illness.

"Dad was standing by Mom. He felt my pulse and told Mom that I was not dead, but he wondered why in thunder Doctor Sam hadn't arrived to give me something for the pain.

"I thought again of the doctor, and I could see him pulling up in front of our house at that very minute. I followed him up the walk, and I was able to see him ring the bell. At the same time, I could see my father running down the steps to answer the door.

"Below me, I could hear Mom crying, and I watched as Dad put his arm around her shoulders to comfort her. I thought again of that really terrific prayer that Mom had asked of God. She had really said how much I meant to her and how she had always been true to her inner belief in His power, glory, and grace even if she didn't go to church that often anymore. She had literally begged God to let me live."

From her unique all-seeing perspective, Amy could "see" or "know" what Dr. Pergande was thinking. "He frowned and he took a syringe out of his bag. I could hear what he was saying to himself: 'A good jolt of this will bring her around! She's been into those damn green apples again! Just when I was going to relax with a beer and watch football, I have to come over and take care of this silly, undisciplined kid. And there's no way I'm going to let Bill win our next tennis match!'"

At the same time, Amy was once again touched by her mother's internal monologue: "Please, dear God, don't take my Amy's life. If you must take a life, take mine instead. Or maybe take ten years off my life. Twenty years. Whatever you want, I'll trade it for my baby's life."

Amy was completely shaken by her mother's offer to barter her own life to God in exchange for Amy's. "There was no way that I could let Mom do such a thing," she said. "It was as if I somehow visualized myself taking a running jump for my body, and I believe that I actually heard a kind of thumping sound, like someone hitting the mattress hard with an open hand, when I reentered my body. I guess that my arms and legs straightened out, and I halfway sat up, startling Doctor Sam, as well as Mom and Dad.

"Doctor Sam gave me the shot for the pain, and I certainly didn't try to fight it. Just before I fell asleep from the sedative, I tried to tell my parents and Doctor Sam about my strange out-of-body experience. No one seemed to believe me, but Doctor Sam did give me a funny look when I told him not to be too hard on Dad during their next tennis afternoon. I decided not to say anything to Mom about having heard her prayer, but I did hug her, and I told her how much I loved her before I drifted off.

"I was seventeen, and before this experience, I think that I had really started to become a pain in the neck for Mom," Amy said. "My out-of-body experience and having heard Mom's prayer really made me shape up— and we became really close.

"And we still are. I'm really happy that God let me come back into my body without accepting Mom's offer to exchange her life for mine. It would have been sad if she had not been able to see the two granddaughters that I have given her and the grandson that Billy presented for her to spoil. We all hope that we have many, many years left to love each other right here on Earth."

— AMY HARGIS

*M*others come in all sizes and shapes, colors and shades, but one thing all mothers have in common is an instinct to protect and defend their children—just like mothers in the animal world who will call attention to themselves when a predator approaches, even to the point of offering themselves up as a sacrifice to save their offspring.

I remember my mother, Lillian, fondly. Certainly we had our differences, but then, as we know, most children don't always agree with their parents every moment. And there are so many moments to remember that it is difficult to say which are best, but all are helpful and encouraging—such as when in her later years my mother told me that as a child I spoke to her of the angels that I had seen.

With her Cherokee Indian heritage, which her adopted mother helped her to keep in touch with as she grew up, Mother helped me to become aware of the earth as a friend. She told me about clouds and how they can speak to us, and about the wisdom that we can gain from our animal friends. She was always able to listen to my stories of dreams and events that I saw that might happen in the future. She never disparaged the information I told her, but she listened to me. Thus, when others did not understand me, I was not as concerned about it as I might have been, for I knew I had my mother who did understand me and who would stand by me. As a result, I did not close off avenues to inner sensitivities and was better able to tune in to vibrations.

My mother took on her "new cosmic assignment" in her early eighties. She passed away on my birthday. Coincidentally, she had experienced a stroke four days earlier on my sister Katina's birthday. She never did play favorites.

Her caring about us did not stop with her passing to the Other Side. I have received dream/vision communications from her, and it was on a couple of these occasions that I realized that mothers continue to care about their children even when they, as a parent, are no longer on the earth plane and have entered another dimension.

On one occasion, when my husband, Norman, and I were returning to Canada from our winter vacation, our scheduled flight was out of Los Angeles on Air Canada. On the morning of our departure, I was awakened by a dream/vision in which my mother appeared to me with a concerned look on her face. I was aware that the message she gave me was, "This is not a good day to fly."

That was it. A simple message.

Very easy to understand. No possibilities for several vague metaphysical interpretations.

"This is not a good day to fly."

I *heard* it again and then my mother's image faded.

I knew the message must require my immediate, but diplomatic, attention. How was I going to tell Norman? He has had an open mind about all my sixth-sense attunements, and he acknowledges that I have given him good business advice in the past, but this time it involved him in a different way. So when we went to breakfast at our favorite Good Earth restaurant in Pasadena on the way to the airport, I told Norman of my mother's message.

I could see that he immediately put up a defensive "you got to be kidding" mental barrier. However, he was also concerned because he knew of the accuracy he had personally seen related to information I had received psychically in the past. But he firmly advised me to just "forget it." We had to go because it was too late to change the tickets *and* his schedule.

I explained to him that if we took the flight, maybe we just wouldn't have to worry about a schedule from that point on. Silence followed. What to do?

People always say they want to know if something unpleasant or tragic is going to occur so that it can be avoided. But when an intuitive warning actually arrives, it causes an inner conflict for some people.

Lots of thoughts passed through my mind. I suddenly recalled a morning years earlier in San Jose when, upon awakening, I had heard an inner voice say, "Do not take Flight 5." I quickly rebooked for another time and flight. And on that day on Flight 5, the landing gear stuck and the plane was unable to land for quite awhile, thereby causing great stress for the passengers. I had avoided that stressful situation thanks to the inner message that I acknowledged. But now it was different. I was not alone. So, although I was personally thankful for the message from my departed mother—"It is not a good day to fly"—it had created a problem of a magnitude that was growing larger by the moment.

I entered a quick meditation prayer and said thank you for my mother's being able to deliver the information. I wasn't sure what I would do, but I wasn't going to get on that plane unless something meaningful was resolved. I also asked for some directive help—and then I just turned it over to the universe.

After we arrived at L. A. International Airport, we went directly to Air Canada and checked in to fly to Winnipeg, via Calgary. We were advised that the plane was being delayed, and we would not leave on time. We were told that the Air Canada plane, carrying Canadian hockey players, including hockey superstar Wayne Gretsky, aboard, had experienced a landing problem and a tire had blown out. Thankfully, no one was hurt, but there was repair involved.

Actually it turned out to be about four hours of repair, and already my mother's warning, "This is not a good day to fly" had proven to be correct. When we were finally able to fly, we arrived in Calgary, just missing the last flight to Winnipeg. The airlines put us in a hotel for the night, and we left for home early the next morning.

The plane arrived safely and uneventfully at Winnipeg International. As we departed the plane,

Norm looked at me and grinned. "Well, it appears your mother knew what she was talking about. Yesterday was not a good day to fly."

Thankfully, it was not a tragic day.

—CLARISA BERNHARDT

*F*rom the annals of psychical research comes a classic case of the amazing power of a mother's love.

Mrs. Sarah Burton held the letter from her daughter in her hands for several moments before she opened the envelope and read its contents. She had received numerous letters from her daughter in rapid succession over the past few weeks. Would this most recent letter leave her with the same eerie sensation that it had not really been written by Lizzie at all?

Her eyes scanned the handwritten pages rapidly.

Once again, the letter began with the brief apology that, since she had burned her hand on the cookstove, her husband, Jim, would write the letter for her. Then Lizzie went on to dictate incidents of common household activities and to close with an affirmation of her love and an assurance that all was well with her.

In form and content, the letter was nearly identical to the others that Mrs. Burton had received recently. But if all was well with Lizzie, why did this terrible feeling of dread continue to plague her? And why did she keep thinking of that awful dream she had recently had—showing Lizzie in danger.

On that troubled day in 1870, Mrs. Burton brought out pen and paper and sat down to write a letter of her own. This time she would not return her daughter's note. This time she would write a letter to a friend who lived in Lewiston, Maine, the hometown of Lizzie and her husband, James Lowell.

Mrs. Burton began by telling her friend that she had, of late, been troubled by a dream concerning the welfare of her daughter. "I first heard this voice," she wrote, "telling me that I was at some place outside of Lewiston where there are numerous lumber mills. I then realized that I was on a lonely road, leading to a densely wooded area. As I continued on, I saw my daughter Lizzie, and her husband, riding in a buggy. Jim turned the horse off the road onto a byroad that ran alongside the river. For a moment I lost sight of them. When I next saw them, they had left the buggy. Lizzie was sprawled on the ground, pleading with Jim to spare her life. Jim raised his hand, as if to strike her. Then a fog seemed to cover the area, and I woke up."

Mrs. Burton concluded the letter by beseeching her friend to make inquiries about Lizzie, and, if possible, to go to visit her in person.

The anxious mother received word from her friend stating that Lizzie had not been seen in Lewiston for several weeks. She had attempted to visit Lizzie in person, but James Lowell had told her that his wife was not at home.

The report from her friend reinforced Mrs. Burton's fears that all was not well with her daughter. The notes just did not sound like Lizzie, and she could not erase that terrible dream from her mind. She resolved to journey to Lewiston to investigate matters for herself.

James Lowell was visibly startled when he opened the door to admit his mother-in-law.

"Why, Mother Burton." He grinned nervously. "You should have told us that you were planning a visit. If Lizzie had known that you were coming, she never would have gone out of town."

"Lizzie is not here?"

"Why, no, she's visiting a friend."

"It's peculiar that she did not mention that she was planning a trip in one of her letters," Mrs. Burton remarked.

"The trip came up rather suddenly," Lowell explained. He seemed to be having a great deal of difficulty in breathing properly.

"And what of her hand?" Mrs. Burton persisted with her questions. "How long must she use you as her stenographer?"

"Why, actually, that is why she is gone. She went to have her hand looked at."

"The doctor in Lewiston isn't good enough?" Mrs. Burton asked, frowning her annoyance. "What is her doctor's name in this other town?"

"Well, really it is only a good friend who has a healing touch, so to speak."

"What is her friend's name, then?" Mrs. Burton kept on. "And where is Lizzie so that I might join her?"

"Oh, you mustn't do that," Lowell stammered. "I mean, she is to have rest and quiet. Don't worry about Lizzie, Mother Burton. I talked to a man just yesterday who had spoken to her and said that she was feeling much better."

"A man can visit her, and I cannot?" Mrs. Burton scowled.

James Lowell continued with his vague assurances and obvious evasions until Mrs. Burton took her leave of his home. Her next stop was that of the Lewiston marshal. She was now convinced that her daughter had met with foul play at the hands of her husband, and she was going to insist upon an investigation.

The lawman was not impressed by her story. "Ma'am, I can't arrest someone on charges such as these. A dream just doesn't stand up in a court of law as very substantial evidence. Why, I couldn't bring a man in for questioning just because someone saw him murder someone in a dream. I'd have to bring in half the county if that were the case. You go on home. Lizzie will probably turn up in a day or two and be perfectly well and safe."

But *three years* went by before anyone ever found a trace of Lizzie Lowell. Mrs. Burton had long since become totally convinced of the validity of her dream, but the authorities were still without any kind of physical evidence that would allow them to launch an investigation.

Then, in October of 1873, a farmer named Small stumbled across some shiny objects in the grass around an old rotted log. These objects appeared to be a row of buttons.

"I thought it kind of strange that the buttons should

be laying there in such a straight line," Small later testified. "If they had fallen off somebody's clothing, they would have been scattered all over the place. As I looked closer at the buttons, I noticed some rotten cloth underneath. When I kicked the pieces around, I uncovered a human skeleton."

The farmer rushed into the marshal's office at Lewiston and told him of his incredible find. When the body was identified as that of Lizzie Lowell, the lawman remembered with a groan the dream of an anguished mother, which he had been discrediting for three years.

In a sensational nine-day trial, James Lowell was convicted of the murder of his wife and sentenced to be hanged. His lawyers, however, managed to get the sentence commuted.

According to Lowell, his wife had been killed by the bucking of their horse. He had buried her and attempted to maintain the charade with his mother-in-law for fear that his story would not be believed.

Twenty-five years later, James Lowell received a pardon because there had been no actual witness to the alleged murder.

But there had been a dream witness. Until her death, Mrs. Sarah Burton insisted that, while she lay sleeping many miles away, she had seen James Lowell murder her daughter. Even the skeptical were forced to concede that the anxious mother had been able to describe the location of her daughter's unmarked grave three years before it had been uncovered. ☙

*A*lthough she has experienced a number of unusual experiences in her life, Rosemary Lockhart will always remember one that stands far above the rest as the most remarkable of all—the night when her mother's dying prayers summoned Rosemary to her bedside for one final farewell.

It was Valentine's Day 1957. Rosemary; her husband, Milo; and her two-year-old daughter, Janet, were staying with her husband's sister and brother-in-law, Ranae and George Crowder, in Springfield, Illinois, until they could get a place of their own. Rosemary was tired after a long day of job hunting for part-time employment to help pay the mounting bills, and she decided against going to the movies with her husband and nephew.

She retired early but awoke when Milo returned. "What time is it?" she asked.

Milo checked his watch. "It's nine-twenty-five."

Rosemary nodded, repeated the time, rolled over, and went back to sleep. It seemed as if she had just turned over when she suddenly saw an old man with a long white beard dressed in a dark robe standing by the bedside.

"The walls seemed to have disappeared," Rosemary said, "and it was as if I could see outdoors. The old man in the robe looked down at me for a moment, then he reached out his hand to me and said 'Come.'"

She spoke not a word in protest, but placed her hand in his. "I rose from the bed and went with him without question. I glanced down and saw that my nightgown had disappeared, and in its place was a flowing white robe. I knew that the night air was cold, but I was oblivious to it. The old man and I were floating just above the treetops. The sky was filled with stars, and below I could see the lights of towns and cities."

After they had traveled like this for a period of time, Rosemary saw that they were coming closer to the ground, just barely skimming above the sidewalk of some small town. She looked around, seeking some identifying clue as to where they might be. Then she spied a large plate glass window with the name "ALLEN" in large red letters.

Immediately she knew where she was. The window was part of the mining company's store in the small West Virginia town where she had grown up. A few houses and turns later, she and the old man were moving up the steps to her brother Jay's house.

The porch was small, and there was a swing filling up what little space there was. Unavoidably, the two travelers brushed against the swing as they passed, and it struck the wall of the house with a thud.

"The old man in the robe opened the door slightly for me to enter; then he disappeared," Rosemary said.

As she stepped into the room and looked around, she could see her brother Jay and sister-in-law Carole. Her sister Becky was standing near the stairway at the back of the room. Her brother's five-year-old son was sitting on the second step of the stair in his pajamas. Several friends and neighbors were also in the room, as well as a few folks unknown to her.

"I walked to the foot of a bed that stood in the center of the room by the front window. In the bed lay my mother, who opened her eyes and smiled at me."

"Thank God," Rosemary heard her mother say. "I knew you'd come."

"I wanted so very much to talk to Mama," Rosemary said. "But even though I could see and hear everything going on in the room, I didn't seem to be able to say a word. And no one except Mama seemed to be able to see me."

"Rosemary," her mother told her, "I wanted to see you so much, that I begged God to send you to me before I died. Don't you grieve. I'm going to rest. I'll be waiting for you."

Rosemary recalled that although her mother looked frail and weak, she suddenly found the energy to rise into a sitting position in her bed.

"I'm so happy to see you," her mother said. "Always remember to ask God when you need help. He'll never fail you. Now I can die happy."

After her mother had spoken those words, she fell back on the bed.

"A man dressed in a brown overcoat and a brown that went to Mama's bed, felt her pulse, and pulled the sheet up over her head. 'She's dead,' he said in a low voice. I looked up at the clock and saw that it was ten-thirty."

The room dissolved into the confusion of the aftermath of the death of a loved one.

"My brother Jay was so close to me as he went out

the door that I could have touched him," Rosemary said. "But I knew that he would not be able to feel me."

Everyone in the room began to weep. Rosemary's sister Becky fainted, and some neighbors took her to their home so that she might be revived in solitude.

"And then all at once I saw my mother's body lying on something that looked like an ironing board with two men bending over it. I got really upset and agitated about this, although I didn't really know why," Rosemary said. "The men were doing something to Mama's body that I could not see. Whatever it was, though, I knew that I had to stop it.

"I tried to jerk the arm of one man away from Mama's body, but it was evident that I could not be felt. I could not utter a sound, and I could not make my physical presence known. To my deep sadness, I was unable to restrain the two men from doing whatever it was that they were doing to Mama."

And then she was back in bed in Illinois.

"My husband's sister Ranae was washing my face with a cold washcloth, and Milo had my head and shoulders in his arms," Rosemary said. "My nightgown was wet with sweat, and my hair was damp from it. I was very cold and weak. But the first thing I asked when I was able to speak was the time. It was nine-thirty-five."

Rosemary immediately informed her husband and

sister-in-law that her mother was dead. She told them that she had seen her die at ten-thirty, West Virginia time.

"No one believed me. I was told that I had just had a bad nightmare. Milo said that he had been sitting at the edge of the bed, having a last cigarette before going to bed, when I had begun to moan. Large drops of sweat had formed on my face, and he had called Ranae to help rouse me."

Rosemary was convinced that her mother was dead and that word would come the following morning. After two restless days, anticipating any moment to receive the dreaded news, Rosemary tried calling her brother's home. There was no answer.

It was four days before word came.

"I went to the post office and there was a letter from my brother Jay: 'We tried to get you, Sis, before Mom died. She died on Valentine's Day evening at ten-thirty, and we kept her as long as possible. We sent you a telegram. A big ice storm knocked out our telephone service, so we couldn't call. We buried Mom this evening.'"

The letter was postmarked two days before.

The next morning as Rosemary prepared to travel to her hometown—by more conventional means this time—she received a telegram from the post office: "Mom got pneumonia. Not expected to live. Come at once."

Rosemary said that she would always feel that pain. "For some reason the telegram had been delayed in mailing, and it had arrived too late for me to see Mama alive."

When Rosemary Lockhart arrived in the West Virginia mining town where she had been born and reared, she found that her sister-in-law Carole had cleaned the room in which Mama had died, even to the extent of removing the bed and rearranging the furniture.

Before she would let any of them tell her anything, Rosemary asked her brother to call in a neighbor whom she knew well and who she knew had been present the night of her mother's death.

"I then related my remarkable experience," Rosemary said. "And to verify it, I told them where everyone in the room had been seated or standing and exactly how the furniture had been arranged that night."

When Rosemary completed her amazing account, Carole showed her two boards lying in the backyard. Nailed together, they resembled a crude ironing board. The deceased woman had been prepared for burial in the house, and the boards had been used by the undertakers for the embalming process.

Then Rosemary was able to understand her feelings of disgust toward the men that she had tried to keep from her mother in the strange vision. "Mama had a horror of being embalmed, and once she had made me promise that if I was present when she died, I would not let her body be embalmed."

Jay and Carole told her that Mama had told all those present that she would be able to die happy if she could only see Rosemary one last time.

"Mama had prayed all day that I'd come. Jay and Carole said that just before Mama died, something had hit the front porch swing and it had struck the wall with a loud thud. Right after that, something had opened the front door, even though it was a clear frosty night and no breeze was stirring. Jay had closed the door just after Mama had died.

"They told me, too, that just before Mama had died, she suddenly sat up in bed and had passed away while she was smiling and talking while looking straight at the foot of the bed. They could catch a word here and there, but thought that she was delirious.

"Did my mother really see me in answer to her dying prayers?" Rosemary asked. "Did my soul leave my body to go out to be with the one who was preparing to take flight to Heaven so that she could die happy? I believe so."

The thrill of exploring nature with one's children can bring with it a very high price tag. Even the most cautious woodland explorer may find herself having to pay dearly.

Irene Govis, thirty-two; her daughter, Nevin, five; her son, Zachary, seven; her neighbor's daughter, Natasha Winch, six; and the Govises' dog, Petie Bear, were hiking to observe a beaver pond in the thickly wooded area outside North Bay, Ontario. They were all excited to have the opportunity to watch the beavers busy at work in their native habitat.

Zachary's enthusiasm got the better of him and he rushed ahead of the others on his bike, just missing a black bear and her cubs that were emerging on the trail after snacking among some berry bushes.

Ever since she had been a child, Irene had been warned never to mess with a mama bear's ultraprotective instinct toward her cubs. She yelled at Zachary to freeze in his tracks. She wanted to stop any sudden movements that might be interpreted as threatening to this big mama's babies.

As Irene turned to reach for little Nevin, however, the bear attacked her from behind, knocking her down, biting and clawing at her flesh. Irene felt terrible pain as the angry bear ripped mercilessly at her thighs and backside.

But far surpassing the pain that she was enduring was the horror that Irene felt when the bear dropped her and lunged for her five-year-old daughter. Irene screamed in anguish and fear when the massive jaws of the enraged creature closed around Nevin's neck, its fangs puncturing her jugular.

That was when Petie Bear charged the bear, snapping and growling at the monster that was mauling and biting the members of its human family. Although the dog was no match for the black bear, Petie Bear distracted the enraged beast long enough for Irene to throw herself protectively on top of her badly injured daughter.

Irene prayed that Nevin would not bleed to death from the slash wounds in her throat before she could get her to the hospital.

And then the bear was once again ripping and biting at Irene's back and the helpless mother wondered for a terrible moment if any of them would survive long enough to get help for their wounds.

At last, the mother bear felt she had exacted enough punishment to compensate for the perceived threat to her cubs and summoned her babies to her side. The three of them crashed off into the bushes from whence they had come.

Although her own wounds were severe and bleeding profusely, Irene, a registered nurse, ripped off her shirt and wrapped it around her daughter's neck to stem the bleeding. Then, calling upon all the reserves that she could muster, she cradled Nevin in her arms and ran with Zachary and Natasha to the nearest home, where the startled owner called an ambulance.

Dr. Paul Preston, who treated the mother and daughter at North Bay Civic Hospital, reported that little Nevin had come within a "millimeter" of death, while Irene had suffered twenty-four puncture wounds.

The powerful force of a mother's love had enabled

Irene Govis to fight off a savage bear to save her children and to use her own body as a shield against its vicious claws and fangs as it tried to kill her little girl.

*J*ust three days before her due date, a very pregnant Christine Tanguay jumped into the ice-covered Yamaska River to save the lives of her two young children.

On March 24, 1996, Christine and her husband, Michel, were loading up their car after having eaten lunch at Michel's parents' home in Adamsville, Quebec. It suddenly occurred to her that she hadn't seen four-year-old Patrick or two-year-old Melanie for a while. Although nine months' pregnant and ready to deliver their third child, Christine went in search of the kids so they could go home.

Something told her to look down by the river. When she did, she felt as if she had been struck by lightning. There, in the middle of the ice-covered river, were the colorful pink, purple, and blue jackets of her two children.

Christine screamed for Michel and began running as fast as she could for the shoreline. From what she could see, Patrick and Melanie were both floating facedown, drowning in the freezing river water.

Thinking only of saving her children, Christine jumped into the icy Yamaska River. Within seconds, the freezing water had soaked through her coat and filled her boots, making her "as heavy as a whale." She knew that if she got swept away in the current of the river or got trapped under the ice, she would drown without having a chance to rescue either Patrick or Melanie. At that particular moment, however, nothing was more important than dragging her children to safety.

Somehow, she managed to reach Patrick. She was alarmed to see that he wasn't breathing. Praying that he could be resuscitated, Christine pulled him over to the edge of the ice where Michel could reach him and pull him out of the river.

Then Christine turned around to swim out to Melanie, at least 25 feet away in the current of the river. Once again, praying as she swam, Christine managed to grab on to her daughter's coat. She turned Melanie face-up and was horrified to see that she appeared completely lifeless.

As Christine neared the shore, Michel and his brother Paul took Melanie from her arms, then began to pull her free of the ice and freezing water. Christine was so exhausted that she knew she would not have been able to climb out of the river on her own.

Michel and Paul gave the children CPR while Christine looked on, praying desperately for a miracle. She breathed a great sigh of relief when Patrick began coughing up water and breathing, but it took nearly twenty terror-filled minutes before Melanie took her first breath.

Later, at the hospital, a doctor told Christine and Michel that because Melanie's body temperature had dropped to seventy-eight degrees in the freezing river, the oxygen demands on her body were lowered, thus helping to protect her from brain damage.

Three days later, right on schedule and none the worse for her frightening ordeal in the ice-covered Yamaska, Christine Tanguay gave birth to their new daughter, Veronique—the third miracle Christine had achieved over three unforgettable days. ✑

*E*arly in her married life,
Sherry Hansen Steiger
was told that it would be
virtually impossible for her ever to conceive, carry, and
give birth to a child. This depressing conclusion was
pronounced by a number of specialists after reviewing
the many tests that they had administered. To their
knowledge, they said, no woman had ever become
pregnant with a metabolic reading anywhere near as low
as hers—and she had several other physical conditions
that more than supported their deduction.

Sherry knew that when and if something was meant

to be, *nothing* would be impossible. Approximately six years after she was first told she could never bear a child, she miraculously conceived.

Sherry felt an immediate bond with the new life within her and began to accept what she had once been told was a belief of the Chinese—that a child has already lived a year when it is born. Suspecting the uterine walls and surroundings to be vulnerable to "noise penetration" and not at all "soundproof," Sherry considered that everything within and without could affect the development of the unborn child. She knew this included her thoughts, moods, and interactions with others; the foods she ate, the books and periodicals she read, and the things she saw and heard would all affect the developing child within her.

Sherry implemented as much as possible a positive, constructive attitude, as well as the proper food and nutrition for her unborn son. She just "knew" that the life within was a male child and that his name *had* to be Erik. Later, there were even comments that he was a Viking about to be reborn—and in the later portion of her pregnancy, Sherry joked that he must still be wearing his horned headgear!

As a part of their seminary training at the Lutheran School of Theology in Chicago, Sherry and her husband, Paul, were assigned to undertake a summer ministry in

Wisconsin Dells, Wisconsin. This would mean several moves during the time of pregnancy—and about an eighteen-hour workday, seven days a week. The living quarters for the ministers were located in a historic home and consisted of a single room and a porch, with occasional use of the kitchen and a shared bathroom with the owner of the home, a gentlewoman in her eighties.

The young ministers' major project of the summer was the creation of the Jawbone, a coffeehouse that would introduce a new ministerial concept, an ecumenical effort from the ground up—which also meant that it had to be constructed and readied before the ministerial outreach to the area teenagers could even begin. Board by board, they would have to erect walls, ceilings, and the stage, then paint the donated chairs and tables.

All in all, this was a wonderful way to build a service ministry, but not such a wonderful way to build a child. And in addition to her many officially assigned duties, Sherry had taken in her younger brother, Paul Jr., who was going through a difficult period of rebellion.

Doing the best she could under the circumstances, Sherry continued to talk to the developing child in her womb. She made light of the practice at first. So she would not seem too "loony," she would make comments like "Erik, did you hear that?" or "Oops, sorry that was so loud!" Soon the kids who hung out at the Jawbone were talking to Erik as well.

Sherry received many interesting confirmations that the child within her was responding in surprising ways to the various outer stimuli. Thinking at first that it must be coincidence, Sherry noticed what seemed to be kicks to her abdomen in perfect time to the music being performed on the coffeehouse stage. When the kicking continued with startling regularity, she was soon convinced that the flawless timing of the kicks to match the beat of the music was anything but coincidence.

It didn't take long for the word to spread among the kids, the other ministers, and the lay volunteer chaperones, and they soon were all feeling Erik's "drumbeat" and calling him the prodigy drummer boy.

Erik was born October 9, 1967, one month early. As soon as he was mobile, his favorite toys were pots and pans that he dragged from a cupboard, lined up like a drum set, and beat on with wooden spoons. Even at the beach he preferred coffee cans, bottles, or shells turned upside down to any toy—and he always beat out a perfect beat to the music he made. It was not surprising that his favorite song was "The Little Drummer Boy."

While Sherry's theories might have seemed quaint and charming but largely constituted of coincidence and wishful thinking in the 1960s, since that time there have been numerous studies conducted that demonstrate that she was correct in believing that the unborn child in her womb was responding to the beat of the music around them. Most recently, in July 2001, psychologist Alexandra Lamont of the University of Leicester in Great Britain released the findings of Leicester's research group showing that babies can recognize tunes they have heard in the womb even a year after birth. Whether their moms play Mozart or The Backstreet Boys before the babies are born, long after their birth they will continue to show a preference for that music.

According to Dr. Lamont, researchers have known that the fetus is able to hear fully only twenty weeks after conception. "Now we've discovered that babies can remember and prefer music that they heard before they were born," she said (*The Guardian,* July 11, 2001). "After the babies were a year old they heard the prenatal music and other music matched for style, key, pace, and loudness." Such experiences, Dr. Lamont concluded, indicate that mother and baby can share early experiences, "even before they have a chance to meet."

When he was director of the dream lab at Maimonides Medical Center in Brooklyn, New York, Dr. Stanley Krippner told Brad Steiger that a large percentage of pregnant women have dreams in which something will go wrong with their unborn child. Expectant mothers often describe their babies as being born deformed or possessed of unusual or grotesque attributes. And they had those dreams long before *Rosemary's Baby* became a best-selling novel and a popular motion picture. Because so many mothers have such dreams, researchers consider them to be natural fears and in most cases do not believe them to be pathological.

Research conducted at the dream lab by Diana R. Schneider, with the cosponsorship of Dr. William Pomcranre, director of the Maimonides Hospital obstetrics department, determined that pregnancy, the wish for pregnancy, and the fear of pregnancy actually influence dream content to a high degree. For example, Dr. R. L. Van de Castle, research consultant to Schneider's project, found that, occasionally, a woman might have a dream that accurately foresees the future in regard to her pregnancy and her delivery.

Dr. Van de Castle described the experiences of one woman who had had recurring nightmares for several years, ever since she had seen illustrations of an abnormal fetus in her fiance's medical textbook. The woman said that her dreams were always the same. She lay in bed in hard labor. Her sister was always in the dream, and she, too, was in the terminal stages of gestation. The dream always ended the same way. Her sister would give birth to a healthy, normal child, and the dreamer, after long, excruciating labor, would bear a deformed baby.

The woman suffered through these awful dreams for nearly six years before she married and became pregnant for the first time. Then she knew, instinctively and absolutely, that the pregnancy would repeat itself identically with the dream, she told Dr. Van de Castle. And it did, even to her sister actually being pregnant at the same time that she was. As in the recurring dream, the woman's sister gave birth to a healthy, normal girl, while she bore a deformed stillborn child.

When the woman became pregnant again a year later, her doctor warned her to expect a psychologically difficult pregnancy because of her previous experience. But the woman assured her doctor that now that the dream had lived itself out in reality, there would be no more worry on her part. The dream never recurred, and she gave birth to a normal child. ☙

*L*isa Padwin's precognitive dream had a happier message, and because the young woman believed in its declaration, she saved the life of her unborn child.

She was in her second month of pregnancy when her doctor advised her that she must have an abortion. In the doctor's opinion, it would be fatal for her to bear the child. At her husband's urging, Lisa made the necessary arrangements to be aborted legally.

Then, the night before the abortion, she had a dream in which an angel appeared before her holding a handsome baby boy in its arms. On the strength of that dream, Lisa Padwin refused the abortion and carried the baby full term.

Seven months later, she gave birth to the healthy, smiling baby boy she had seen so vividly in her dream with absolutely no risk to her own well-being. ☙

When Judy Fitzgerald was pregnant, she and her husband lived with in-laws, an arrangement that she charitably described as "an unhappy situation." Whenever she had a particularly trying day at work or at home attempting to remain calm and in balance amidst bickering, she would experience the same beautiful dream in which she was walking among lovely flowers with a little girl at her side, listening to soothing, uplifting, inspirational music playing in the background.

After her little girl Maureen was born, and they

moved into a home of their own, the beautiful dream ceased, but Judy often thought of it. When her daughter was about five, Judy took her along to a flower show being held at a convention hall. The entire hall had been transformed into a lovely, fragrant garden, and a live orchestra was playing soothing, uplifting music.

Suddenly it struck her. This was her beautiful dream. The marvelous, tension-relieving dream that she had had when she was pregnant. The therapeutic dream that had kept her sane while living in "an unhappy situation."

The most remarkable facet of her shock of recognition occurred when little Maureen tugged at her skirt with eyes sparkling and said excitedly, "We've been here lots of times before, haven't we, Mommy?"

Our scientists have only begun to explore the many subtle, unconscious links that exist between the expectant mother and the child she nurtures in her womb.

*L*oving mom Julie Christine was faced with one of the most difficult decisions that any mother could ever be asked to make — to place her son's fate in the hands of God and authorize the doctors to shut down his life-support system.

Two weeks before, her son, twenty-year-old John Martin, had been struck by a car while crossing the street in San Rafael, California. His head had gone through the windshield, and from the very beginning, the doctors had held out little hope for his recovery.

While it is said that such tragedies often come in

pairs, this was becoming almost too much for any one person to absorb, for Julie had just come from the bedside of her twenty-three-year-old daughter Eileen, who had been seriously injured in a head-on crash near her home in North Carolina. Once Eileen appeared to be off the critical list and on the path of recovery, Julie had returned to California to find her son lying near death and on life-support machines.

Despite two surgeries, John remained in a coma, unresponsive for two weeks. Doctors discussed his options for recovery. They could attempt a third surgery, but they stated frankly that the outcome at this stage appeared to be very bleak.

Julie spent many hours debating John's medical options. Perhaps her angels would answer her prayers as they had when John was born. He had suffered from jaundice at birth and his health was so bad that the doctors had advised her that little Johnny might never leave the hospital. But he did, and he had grown up to be a robust and vigorous young man.

But now, Julie sat at her son's bedside, tears flowing freely over her cheeks. How it grieved her to see her handsome young son lying there, head swathed in bandages, not even aware of her presence, perhaps not even conscious of his own existence. Would another surgery improve his condition? Or, as the doctors had frankly admitted, be of no benefit at all.

Julie made her decision. Out of the deepest love for her son, she gave the doctors permission to discontinue the life-support system. She knew that, ultimately, God would decide her son's fate.

As she sat at John's bedside, waiting for his last breath, praying for his peaceful release from suffering, she whispered her love to him: "I carried you in my womb twenty years ago, and now I'll carry you in my heart forever."

Julie bent her head in prayer, so oblivious to her external surroundings that it took her a moment or two to realize that someone was gently stroking her hair.

She sat up, startled and joyous to see that it was the hand of her son that had brushed her hair. Miraculously, he appeared to be emerging from the coma that had enveloped him for two weeks.

"I love you," Julie cried, stunned at his sudden recovery.

At the sound of her voice, John opened his eyes, looked into his mother's loving face, and mouthed the words right back.

When John's father, John Martin Sr., who lives in Pennsylvania, arrived, he was thankful to see that his son was fighting once again for his life. He had rushed to the California hospital after leaving their daughter's bedside in North Carolina, uncertain if John would be alive by the time he arrived.

Dr. Merrill Nisam, critical care director at Marin General Hospital, cautioned that the full effect of John's injuries would not be known for many months, but his miraculous recovery from the coma had certainly given everyone reason to be extremely hopeful. "[John Martin] has his youth, the medical care given him since he was injured—and great support from his family," Dr. Nisam said [*Examiner*, March 14, 1995].

And we might well add that John also had the unconditional gifts of his mother's love. ♡

*S*he felt just like Dorothy in *The Wizard of Oz*, Chanta Adams said, after a tornado lifted her and her two infant sons from their home and deposited them on some tree branches 50 feet away.

The tornado had been spun out of Hurricane Bertha, and on July 13, 1996, it devastated the tiny town of Edwardsville, Virginia, near Chesapeake Bay. Twenty-two-year-old mother Chanta Adams was lying on her queen-sized bed, sleeping between her sons Javonte, two, and Trevaughn, fifteen months, when she was suddenly awakened by a loud roaring sound, as if a freight train

were bearing down on them. Chanta screamed for her
sixteen-year-old cousin, Khalif, to run into the bedroom,
but just then the side of their mobile home blew out and
he was blown away like a dried leaf and carried toward
the woods.

Chanta instinctively wrapped her arms around her
sons as the violent twister lifted the queen-sized bed with
them on it and spun it around and around until they
were three stories high, spinning crazily in the center of
the howling winds.

Chanta said later that the three of them were being
tossed around as if they were rubber balls, and she kept
praying for God to let them down, *gently, please, gently.*

And then her prayer was granted. They landed
among the broken branches and rain-drenched trees
50 feet from the spot where their home had once been.
Amazingly, all three of them were still on the mattress,
a son on either side of his mother.

Capt. Thomas Neale of the Northumberland
(Virginia) County Sheriff's Department declared Chanta
Adams and her children among the luckiest people in the
world to survive being carried aloft by a tornado.
Although they didn't escape without a scratch—Chanta
required twenty-six stitches in her scalp; two-year-old
Javonte suffered a broken collarbone, a fractured skull,
and a broken eye socket bone; and fifteen-month-old

Trevaughn had minor scrapes and bruises—the Adams family readily agrees that they experienced a miracle. God was indeed looking out for them.

And what about cousin Khalif, who was blown out of the side of the mobile home as if he were a dried leaf in the wind? He escaped with only a cut on his back, so he, too, must have had a guardian angel on his shoulder. ◎

The Dwyer family used to sit up half the night discussing the paranormal and life after death. Adam Dwyer said that their mother, Bernice, was a strong believer in the continuation of the human personality beyond the grave, and she felt certain that throughout her life she had received many positive proofs that deceased loved ones had made contact with her from beyond the grave. Adam; his wife, Marcia; and his sister Crystal and her husband, Frank, would drink cup after cup of coffee and sometimes stay up until nearly dawn. They enjoyed sharing accounts of the

mysterious and the unknown, and listening to their
mother tell of the times when she was certain that she
had received spirit contact.

"One of these contacts had to do with our father,"
Adam said. "Dad, Ernie Dwyer, a merchant seaman, had
been washed overboard while working on an ore boat in
Lake Superior when I was only ten and my sister Crystal
was seven. His body had never been found, but Mom
assured us that his spirit had communicated with her and
said that he was at peace. He also said that he would be
watching over us just as long as he could. Then, just after
Crystal graduated from high school and I was home from
college for the occasion, Mom said that Dad had told her
that he was now going to move on into the Light."

Adam confessed that he had never been a strong
believer in life after death when he was a boy. "I kept
wondering why Dad never appeared to me or to Crystal,
only to Mom. As I grew older, I began to suspect that the
messages that she claimed to receive from Dad were only
some kind of wish fulfillment on her part."

Bernice Dwyer had been reared a strict Methodist,
so there probably never was a time in her life when she
didn't believe in the existence of the soul and the promise
of life eternal. After her husband had disappeared in the
icy waters of Lake Superior when she was a thirty-three-
year-old mother with two children to raise, she began

reading books on the supernatural, psychical research, mediumship, and metaphysics. Although she remained a sporadic churchgoer, her full-time job at a manufacturing plant and part-time job as a waitress at a truck stop often left her too tired on Sunday mornings to get herself and her kids into their "go-to-meeting" clothes. More and more she found the proof of life after death that she needed by reading about the scientific approach to the subject employed by modern parapsychologists.

"I certainly did not *disbelieve* in life after death," Adam said, "but I, personally, had no evidence to prove it to my satisfaction."

That changed in autumn 1978, when he was thirty years old, teaching high school in New Hampshire, and visiting his mother in Minnesota over Thanksgiving vacation with his new bride, Marcia.

"We were sleeping in my old room, and I was awakened about 4:30 in the morning by loud rapping noises coming from the guestroom," Adam said. "For some reason, I was momentarily seized by a sense of fear as the rapping sounds continued."

Prompted to investigate the disturbance by his wife, who was trying to fall back to sleep, Adam walked downstairs to see if the old furnace was making the noises. Even though the rappings seemed to be coming from the guestroom, it made more sense that it was just the furnace kicking in against the November chill.

He was surprised to find his mother sitting at the kitchen table with tears streaming down her cheeks. Before he could express his concern, she answered his unspoken question. "It's your aunt Laurie, my dear, dear sister," she said. "She's just passed away."

Adam was taken aback and sorrow washed over him. Aunt Laurie was a tall, blond bundle of nonstop energy. When he was little, he had thought she looked like a movie star. And she was so young. He knew his mother was fifty-three, so Laurie, the younger sister, was only around forty-nine. "I . . . I didn't even know Aunt Laurie was ill," he said.

"She wasn't. It was an accident. She was driving unfamiliar and icy roads too fast and went over an embankment."

Adam felt tears sting his eyes. "My God, how terrible. I . . . I didn't hear the telephone ring. Who called?"

His mother poured a fresh cup of coffee and offered it to him. "No one called. Didn't you hear the rapping noises coming from the guest room?"

Adam had momentarily forgotten what had gotten him out of bed. "Yes, I heard the rapping sounds."

"That was Laurie come to say goodbye," his mother said matter-of-factly. "You know how she and Max liked that room when they would come to visit. Well, once she got me awake with the rapping, she told me what had happened and said she would see me again with Ernie and Grandma and Grandpa and Uncle Max in the other world."

Adam accepted the cup of coffee and joined his mother at the table. "Mom, I don't mean to be rude, but . . ."

That was as far as he got in his protestations that his mother's imagination had run away with her. The telephone rang. It was a police officer in Montana notifying Bernice Dwyer, listed as Laurie Cameron's next of kin, that her sister had been killed in an accident that morning. She had been driving at excessive speeds on icy roads and had slid over an embankment to her death. Time of death: approximately 3:30 Mountain Time; 4:30 Central.

Adam had now received proof that the human spirit survives physical death. From that time on, during visits back home with his mother, he could discuss psychical research on a much freer basis.

On July 17, 2000, a loud crash jolted Adam Dwyer out of his sleep.

"I sat up and listened, but I could hear no other strange sounds emanating from any corner of our bedroom," Adam said. "The only discernible sound was the steady breathing of Marcia lying beside me. I looked at the illuminated alarm clock on the nightstand. It was two o'clock. Our two sons, Ray, eighteen, and Ron, twenty, both had jobs as counselors at the same summer camp that they had attended when they were kids. We were home alone.

"I kept thinking that the sound had come from our closet, that something must have toppled over and crashed to the floor, but finding no evidence of such a fall, I assumed that I had been dreaming. I lay back down and dozed off."

Adam had scarcely nestled back into sleep when a loud rapping sound began. This time he was certain that the raps were coming from the closet.

"As soon as I would sit up, the rapping would cease. When I lay back down, it would begin again, seemingly louder than before," Adam recalled.

"What's making that weird noise?" Marcia asked, no longer able to sleep through the persistent rapping. "Honey, it seems to be coming from our closet."

The two of them went to investigate, turning on the light, moving boxes, lifting Adam's heavy hiking shoes, checking Marcia's running shoes.

"Something was pounding somewhere in this room," Marcia declared adamantly. "I'm going to keep looking until I find out what it was."

"Sweetie," Adam cautioned her. "It's three o'clock. I've already been looking for the source of the raps for an hour. And Mr. Alarm Clock is going to scream at us to be up for work at six-forty-five!"

Marcia reconsidered. There appeared to be nothing out of the ordinary, so maybe it would be better to catch a few more winks before the alarm went off.

They had barely settled back down in bed when the rappings started again.

"That's when I finally remembered about Aunt Laurie and the rappings in the guest room back home," Adam said. "The moment that I said aloud, 'Oh, my God! It's like when Aunt Laurie's spirit rapped on the guest room walls,' the noises ceased."

Marcia put her arms around him. "Oh, honey," she paused, picking her words carefully, "could it be . . . your mom? You've been so concerned about her heart problems."

Adam had been struggling with that same uncomfortable question. It was a few minutes after two in Minnesota—much too late to call his mother to check in on her.

When their bedroom telephone rang at that moment, both Adam and Marcia jumped back from it as if it were some hidden enemy about to attack them. It was Crystal, speaking the dreaded words that Adam always knew that he would one day have to hear.

It was obvious that she had been crying, so he, too, began to weep before she had spoken one word: "Adam, it's Mom. She suffered a major heart attack after dinner. She had eaten out with her friend, Mrs. Sorenson, who called me. Mom passed away at the hospital at one o'clock."

And then Crystal apologized for being unable to speak any further, saying that they would talk later. Adam heard her crying as she hung up. And then he and Marcia spent the next several hours comforting one another.

On the flight into the Minneapolis–St. Paul airport, Adam thought of his beloved mother and the way in which she had contacted him to prepare him for the shock of her passing. "Once again, Mom had given me proof of survival after physical death," he said.

When the taxi dropped Adam, Marcia, and their sons off at Crystal and Frank's home, his sister opened the door and quickly ushered them inside. Her eyes were red from weeping, but she greeted them with unparalleled joy. Adam was a bit disconcerted, considering all the arrangements that had yet to be made.

Crystal saw that everyone was seated comfortably, and then she described how she had gone into their living room the previous night after she had returned from the hospital and the bedside of their mother. "I wanted to sit beneath a painting that Mom had given us for Christmas a few years ago," she began. "You know, Adam, your family got the same painting, the one of Jesus standing at the door, knocking to be admitted."

Adam and Marcia nodded at the reminder. "We grew up with the same painting in Mom's house," Adam said.

"Since the painting meant so much to Mom, I sat beneath it praying," Crystal went on, "praying for comfort and some sign of Mom's spiritual ascension. After only a few minutes of praying, I was startled by a knocking on the wall beside the painting and then the painting fell off the wall."

Adam interrupted to say how he and Marcia had been awakened by a knocking in their bedroom and eventually understood it to be their mother's signal that she had passed.

Crystal smiled in recognition and continued. "There was a piece of paper between the glass and the backing of the frame. I saw a sheet of Mom's familiar stationery, and I saw that it was a note from her, which I wish to share with the entire family at this time: 'To my dear children: Know that I will always be with you, whether it is in this life or the next, and remember that love is the greatest power in the universe. Love, Mom.'"

Adam concluded his account by stating that Bernice

Dwyer had given her children and grandchildren the most precious gift of a mother's love imaginable—an unshakable faith that the soul and the power of love continue even after death.

When his mother passed away on February 23, 1999, Roger Emerson was left with feelings of unresolved guilt in addition to his grief.

"For the last two or three years of her life, Mom, Estelle Emerson, had been behaving in a very strange and irritating manner, making it very difficult to be patient with her," Roger said. "At first my sister Lois and I thought Mom had Alzheimer's or some other mentally degenerative affliction. She seemed very absentminded and her memory was terrible. It seemed as though she had historically revised every major event in our lives to make my sister and I appear to be wretched children who were always trying to take advantage of our parents.

"I suppose the most difficult aspect of Mom's personality change was that she had always been so pleasant and understanding when we were children," Roger continued. "She had always been the perfect mom—as ideal a mother as the ones on television. Beaver and Wally Cleaver had nothing on us. Our mom could out-mom Barbara Billingsley or even Donna Reed."

And then, Roger explained, it seemed as though their once perfect mother, who never complained and who was always pleasant, literally changed overnight into a fault-finding, nit-picking, never-satisfied, always irritable mother.

"Although I know it troubled her, I stopped taking my kids to see their grandmother," Roger said. "I just didn't want them to have memories of their grandmother as some totally unpleasant person. My kids, Meg, three, and Derek, five, were younger than Lois' daughter, Kris, who was seventeen and could form some perspective about Grandma Emerson's deteriorating mental condition. My wife, Kerry, had refused to visit months before, for she seemed particularly to provoke a foul mood and nasty insults from Mom, who accused her of having allowed herself to become pregnant to snare me.

In actuality, we had been married two years before Derek was born. Kerry, however, remained understanding and encouraged me to visit Mom as often as I wished."

A medical examination ruled out Alzheimer's, so Lois, who was nearly six years older than Roger and who had even more cherished memories of a loving, cheerful mother, insisted that perhaps their mother had a brain tumor.

Or, Roger had resigned himself to considering maybe their mother had suddenly begun to reveal a mean streak, a nasty side of herself that she had somehow managed to keep hidden until their father's death four years ago. "You know, her dramatic personality change occurred about a year after Dad's death," Roger reminded his sister. "Maybe she had this side of herself all these years but Dad's tranquil nature kept her balanced."

Lois readily conceded that their father had an exceptionally well-balanced personality, but she remembered her parents as very evenly matched in terms of their endearing personal characteristics. "It has to be a brain tumor," she argued. "What else could alter our mother's personality in such a manner?"

Roger's friend, Dr. Peter West, a psychologist at the local college, advised him to be more accepting of his mother's change of character. Some folks simply did become a bit more crotchety and impatient with younger people—especially their own children—as they got older. Roger had to remember that his mother was eighty-two. And perhaps his father's death did have a great deal to do with her becoming angry and upset with the world.

"From what I understand," Dr. West pointed out, "your folks were married before they were out of their teens, and, as a couple of scared but adventuresome kids, they left their small town in Nebraska and moved to a suburb of Chicago to seek their fortunes, so to speak. They lived and worked hard together for nearly ten years before they had Lois, their first child. Your parents were a solid unit, devoted to one another. Except for the years when your mother stayed home to look after the kids and your father went off to work, they were never apart for more than a couple of hours. Neither one of them had any hobbies or activities that took them away from each other. They were completely realized and completed in one another. After all those years of such bliss and happiness, she could very well now feel robbed, cheated. The great love of her life has been taken from her, leaving her with two kids who visit her only when it is convenient and who act upset because their mom is no longer June Cleaver."

Roger admitted that his friend's advice made some kind of sense, so he tried to approach his mother with a new understanding.

"But it was hard to be patient when Mom's once even disposition had been replaced by a temperament that was easily irritated and could blaze forth at a moment's notice into awful temper tantrums over the most minute of circumstances," he said.

And then the awful moment came one Sunday afternoon when Roger was visiting his mother at their family home.

"I should have waited until some afternoon later in the week," he recalled. "I had a terrible headache and felt a miserable cold coming on. To make matters worse, it had been a horrible week at work, and I had a major presentation to deliver first thing in the morning. When Mom lashed out at me for having broken her favorite brush with the mirror on the back, I wondered why I was wasting my precious time with her hateful self when I should be home working on my notes. She kept screaming at me for being so disrespectful of her personal possessions, on and on. Now, you must understand that I had broken that mirror when I was six years old, and I had tearfully and profusely apologized to Mother, who at the time had accepted the accident as totally inconsequential in the flow of life occurrences. When she kept on and on with it all these many years later, I lost my temper."

Roger said that he struck back with some nasty words and some cruel barbs of his own. He called his mother crazy and threatened to place her in a home. With that he stormed out of the house, shouting back over his shoulder that he might never return, that he didn't want to see her ever again.

"And I never did see her again," Roger said solemnly. "At least not in life. Two weeks later, Mom died of a brain tumor."

On the night following his mother's death, Roger lay in awful sleeplessness, tortured with thoughts of recrimination. There had been so many good times in his earlier life with his mother, why couldn't he have allowed those memories to have sustained him during the trying days of his mother's tragic personality change?

"Death can be a very stern teacher," Roger said. "The Grim Reaper presents too many lessons that are too late to correct. I now saw clearly how faulty human judgments can be. I perceived with great sorrow how a quickly uttered word can leave an indelible impression on the psyche. Most of all, I realized how Mom's irascibility late in her life was due to some unfathomable cause that lay beyond the rational mind and its compulsion to find reasons for everything in life. I felt a terrible guilt for not having had the strength of soul to remain more patient with Mom."

So that he would not disturb his wife, who had somehow managed thus far to remain asleep as he tossed and turned, Roger went downstairs to sit quietly with his painful thoughts in the darkened living room.

"I had just begun to sob aloud in my despair when I distinctly felt a kiss on my left cheek," Roger said. "I turned quickly, expecting to see Kerry come to comfort me, and I saw the faint form of Mom standing beside me.

"She was smiling, and she looked very much the way that I remembered her when I was a little boy of around six or seven. I sat bolt upright in my recliner chair, and Mom's lovely, smiling image leaned forward and kissed me once again on my left cheek. I felt that kiss, warm and loving, as vividly as I had ever felt it in her living form. And then Mom's image vanished.

"But her smile and her kisses had told me that she, too, was sorry about our strained relationship during her final years. She had forgiven me for my harsh words. In the place, the dimension, the heaven, where she now was, she had received a much larger perspective. And now I, too, must forget about those awful times in her declining years and remember only the wonderful times that we enjoyed in the past. And knowing that she had forgiven me for my impatience and cruel outburst, I must now forgive myself.

"I am well aware of how many people in our

materialistic and skeptical world will explain away the kiss of forgiveness that I received from the spirit of my mother; but for me, the sensation of that kiss was too real, too genuine, too filled with the pure gifts of a mother's love for me to doubt."

*S*he may not have believed in miracles before that fateful day in 1996, but when Michelle Markotan's twenty-three-month-old son, David, fell from a seventh-floor window and survived, she knew the sky had to have been filled with angels.

Little David had been playing near an open screened window when he suddenly leaned against the mesh and it gave way. Becky, his three-year-old sister, came running into the kitchen where their mother was working and screamed that the baby had just fallen out the window.

Michelle was "scared to death" when she entered the room and saw the ripped screen. Then, when she rushed to the window to look down, she was horrified when she saw David lying on the ground seven floors below. Instinctively, she cried out to God not to take their son from them.

David Sr., who was outside working on their car, was puzzled by the sound of a "thud" about 30 feet away from him. When he investigated and saw his precious son lying motionless, blood trickling from his mouth, he picked David up and began crying.

Miraculously, little David was still breathing. There was at least some hope that he might live if he were rushed to a hospital and received immediate medical treatment—and most likely, serious surgery.

A trauma team was standing by when the ambulance arrived at Pittsburgh's Children's Hospital, ready to rush David into surgery—but the miracle was not yet complete.

Dr. Edward Barksdale Jr., a pediatric surgeon, had expected to face a tragic death of a child or, at the least, a child who had suffered severe life-threatening injuries. However, when he examined David, Dr. Barksdale found that neither likelihood presented itself. The little boy who had fallen seven stories to the ground below had suffered only a slight concussion, a few fractured ribs, and some bruises.

David's father expressed his gratitude to his son's guardian angels, and his mother said she now believes that miracles do most certainly occur.

Dr. Barksdale agreed. "There can be no other explanation," he told reporter Chris Rodell (*National Enquirer*, August 13, 1996). "It's a miracle this boy is alive."

*I*n 1982, times had grown very hard for the Franzen family of Colorado. When Harland, the breadwinner of the large family, was almost fatally injured at work, his wife, Karen, was left with the sole responsibility of providing for six children—all under the age of seventeen.

"Harland's employer was underinsured, and we had absolutely no insurance of our own," Karen Franzen said. "What money we did receive didn't last long after all the medical bills had been deducted. Harland was left bedridden, and we didn't know at that time if he would ever be able to walk, to say nothing of being gainfully employed, ever again. I was a thirty-seven-year-old high school graduate with practically no work experience outside of the home. What kind of job could I get that would be able to bring us enough money to keep our heads above water financially?"

Jason, their seventeen-year-old son, picked up as many small part-time jobs as possible.

"Jason wanted desperately to be able to help his dad and me support the family," Karen explained. "He had always been a really conscientious boy, and when he saw that his part-time jobs just weren't helping all that much, he insisted on dropping out of high school in his senior year and looking for full-time employment."

Karen and Harland would not listen to such a proposition. Somehow, they told Jason, the family would get by on the money that Karen was making as a part-time short-order cook and the dollars that Jason was bringing home with his several small jobs.

But then came the terrible day when they found the money and the note that Jason had left behind.

"He said that he could not stand being unable to help us more," Karen said. "Since he was the oldest, he wrote that he was going to strike out on his own and try to get a good job in a larger city. He would send every cent home that he could. In the meantime, he was leaving behind his special little nest egg of $35.10."

Karen and Harland and the rest of the kids were sick with worry. Jason was not a very tall boy, and he didn't weigh more than 135 pounds. He looked even younger than he was. He was naive and trusting—and he would probably be taken advantage of and exploited by too many unscrupulous employers. Or worse, he could easily be victimized by thugs on the road.

Karen, Harland, and the children prayed each night during family devotions for the Lord to keep a safe watch over their Jason. The days passed into months, and no word arrived from their son. The worst part, Karen said, was not knowing whether Jason was alive or dead.

"A thousand dreadful possibilities tormented me," she said. "I prayed to hear from him until it seemed as though my every breath became a prayer."

Incredibly, a year passed without a single word from their son.

And then, one night, eighteen months after Jason had left home, Karen Franzen had a most unusual dream. "It was just too real to have been an ordinary dream. What it really was, we may never be able to understand."

According to Karen's account, she was awakened in the dream by an insistent knocking at their back door. She got out of bed, fastened her bathrobe about her, and made her still-groggy way through to the kitchen.

She opened the door to find a young Mexican boy standing there, shivering with the cold. Before she could say a word, her mysterious visitor spoke in urgent tones: "Your boy is sick. Come quick!"

Without thinking to question him further, Karen motioned the boy, who was about Jason's age, to come inside. For some reason she could not explain, she rushed to gather all of the spare sheets and bath towels in the house. All thoughts of sleep fled as she piled this linen collection into two huge bundles. She took one bundle and handed the other to the boy.

They threw the bundles over their backs and walked out into the night. Karen specifically remembers closing the door quietly behind her, so as not to awaken her husband and children, and then carefully closing the gate so the dog would not follow her.

Then, with the boy leading the way, they started to walk "quickly and with a gliding motion." They hurried through the streets until they reached open country, then ". . . we fairly skimmed over the roads, uphill, downhill, so fast we seemed to fly."

They climbed mountains and crossed them "as if with wings"—then just as quickly, they descended. They crossed rivers as if they stood on tiny canoes "that scooted us across the water without even getting our feet wet." Karen often found herself looking down on country that she had never seen before, but had read about in books and magazines.

"The trees were large," she recalled. "And from the wide-spreading branches festoons of gray moss hung down like shimmering veils."

Then the road that they had been following wound up and down, over hummocks and through swamps. Finally, they came to a long, low building.

"Your boy is in there," her Mexican guide said.

And then they were inside, and the lad was leading her up a short, steep stairway, covered with dust and cobwebs. They entered a windowless room, illuminated only by the light from the cracks between the clapboard walls and the broken places in the roof. The place was heavy with a moldy, damp smell.

"Oh, Mom!" Karen heard a familiar voice cry out faintly. "You've come!"

Her heart beating faster, Karen rushed forward to discover her son lying on a bare floor in a far corner of the attic. She fell to her knees, clutching her missing son to her breast, noting with alarm that his body was burning hot and that his face was dry and parched with fever.

"Oh, Mom," Jason moaned. "I'm so sick! I'm so sick with fever."

Karen Franzen lost no time. She turned to the

Mexican youth who had brought her there to ask him to bring buckets of cold water—and quickly. When he left, she got busy gathering refuse from the floor, which she wrapped into a pallet. Then she spread a cool, clean sheet over it.

Although Jason was a full-grown young man, she lifted him like a baby to settle him onto her hastily constructed bed.

By this time, Jason's friend had returned with the cold water. She dipped the towels and sheets one by one into the buckets of cool water, wrung them out lightly, then packed them around Jason's feverish body.

Hours later, she finally relaxed, knowing that the fever had broken. She could tell that the worst of her son's illness was over.

"Go to sleep, son," she said. "You'll get well now."

Without saying another word, Jason drifted immediately into a deep sleep.

Karen sat quietly beside him, holding his hand, until she, too, slept.

She awoke in her own bed, exhausted, every bone in her body aching. Karen was so weary that when she attempted to get out of bed, she found that she could not move. Again and again she made an effort to get out of bed, but she was too exhausted to lift her head from the pillow.

Telling Harland how completely drained of energy she was, she recounted her strange dream. "And don't tell me it was just a nightmare," she warned her husband. "Somehow, I know that I was really there with Jason. Harland, he's sick. I know it. Maybe he's dying. And he is somewhere a long, long way from here."

Harland told her to stay in bed and rest. The girls would help with breakfast and the other daily chores.

Karen rolled over and slept the entire day, barely getting up in time to get to her job.

Two days later, the Franzens received a telegram from a county hospital in another state: "Come quickly. Your son very ill—possible amputation."

Karen borrowed money from her sympathetic employer and boarded a bus for the journey to the little mountain town in Oregon. She found the hospital where Jason was hospitalized, and learned that he had suffered the amputation of a foot. Jason was thrilled to see his mother, and they shared a warm, loving reunion.

One day, several weeks later, after Jason had returned to their home, Karen decided to tell him about the strange dream that she had experienced. Jason listened to the part about the Mexican boy who had knocked at the door, but when she began to describe the bizarre journey, he interrupted her.

"Let me give you some very important background

information here, Mom," Jason said. "The boy's name is Ramon Quintero, but I called him 'No Way.' You know, like, 'No way, José.' I guess, he's saved my life twice now."

Jason explained that shortly after he had left home, he had been eating a sandwich in a fast-food restaurant when he glanced up to see a Mexican boy, about his own age, watching him through the window with such a hungry look that Jason could not bear it. He motioned for him to come inside, and he ordered a sandwich for his companion with the last of his money.

Jason left the restaurant and said goodbye to the boy, who was also wandering the country looking for work.

Later that night, as Jason was walking past an alley in a rough part of town, two thugs jumped out of the darkness and blocked his path. They demanded whatever money he had, his coat, even the shoes that he was wearing.

Suddenly, the young Mexican appeared, pushing himself between Jason and the hoods. "No way," he insisted, brandishing a length of pipe under their noses. "No way you gonna take this boy's money. No way! Now you get away, or I'll clobber you good!"

"Believe me," Jason told his mother, chuckling at the memory of Ramon's fierce defense of him, "those punks hit the road."

His newfound friend had smiled and told Jason: "No

way I let them hurt you, amigo. No way!"

Jason christened his friend, "No Way, Jose," and the two of them teamed up together. When the weather got colder, they decided to work their way south to a warmer climate.

The two teenage boys got as far south as Florida, when one of the devastating hurricanes that periodically rip into the coastal regions hit that southern state. Jason and Ramon had been camping on the beach when a hurricane caught them unexpectedly. A huge wave had reared up and crashed down on them, sweeping them off their feet. Another wave hit them, and they were now at the mercy of the storm.

"Somehow, Ramon got hold of me and managed to pull me onto the beach," Jason said, tears welling in his eyes. "I don't know how he did it, but he got me to a place where I was able to get a good hold on a tree trunk. Just as I turned to see how he was making out, another wave swept him out to sea. I never saw him again. Ramon had saved me . . . then lost his own life."

Afterward, Jason began to work his way back toward Colorado and his parents' home, but when someone offered him a job at a forestry camp in Oregon, the money seemed too good to pass up. Maybe now, for the first time, he would be able to save enough to send home to be of help to the family's financial burdens. He hadn't been able to send any money as he had intended, for he and Ramon had barely survived on the pittances that they had received from doing odd jobs.

Then he had come down with the illness and the terrible fever. He tried to keep working, but one day he had collapsed and had spent the night in the forest, exposed to freezing temperatures. The next morning when Jason's foreman found him, he rushed Jason to the county hospital.

Jason spent most of the time in an unconscious or semiconscious state. Occasionally, he came to enough to realize that he was in a hospital, and that he was so ill he might lose his life. Most of the time, however, Jason's fevered mind visualized himself shut up in some musty, dirty old attic, covered with cobwebs and crawling with spiders.

"I did not want to die," he told his mother. "And, like a frightened little boy, I wanted my mom! Oh, Mom, whenever I could think at all, I wanted you there with me. And I prayed—or tried to pray—that you would come . . . that somehow God would send you to me so that you could take care of me."

Jason knew that he had left his physical body on numerous occasions. "I could see my body below me, and I knew that I was dying."

Then one night, he had awakened to find No Way

standing at his bedside. "Amigo, it does not go so well for you. What can I do to help you?"

Although one level of his consciousness knew very well that his friend was dead, Jason unhesitatingly accepted the reality of Ramon's being there, seeking, as always, to be of service. "Please, No Way," Jason asked, "bring my mom to me. Please, No Way, please. As fast as you can!"

Jason fell into a semiconscious state and found himself back in that depressing attic, lying on the bare floor, surrounded by refuse and debris. The place was damp and smelly—and he knew that he was sicker than ever before. And then before his painfully burning eyes, he saw Ramon enter the attic with his mother.

Jason described to his mother all she had done that night to save him, and how Ramon had worked to help her. Finally, he had heard his mother tell him to sleep, and he had drifted into the sweet oblivion of a healing slumber.

He had awakened in a hospital, where a nurse stood taking his pulse. And he was at last rational enough to give her his parents' address in Colorado.

Karen and her son compared the dates of their two extraordinary experiences and they found them to be the same. The night that she had had her bizarre "dream" had been the night that Jason had passed the critical stage of his illness. He had awakened that morning with a normal temperature, thus encouraging the medical personnel to proceed with the required surgery.

"Jason has always insisted that some way or somehow, I was actually there with him that night he was so near death," Karen concluded her account. "And I wholeheartedly agree. His dear friend, Ramon Quintero, had come from Beyond to bring me to my son's side."

*N*ever underestimate the miracle power of a mother's prayer. The night before two-year-old Hays Burton fell eight stories from a balcony onto an asphalt parking lot, his mom, Velmarie, had asked God to send down guardian angels to watch over him.

On August 7, 1993, Velmarie Burton; her seven-year-old son, Drew; three-year-old daughter, Ann Claire; two-year-old Hays; and two of the kids' friends, arrived at a condominium in Destin, Florida, for a family vacation. Greg Burton had to stay behind to work for a few more days, but he planned to join his wife and children as soon as possible.

That night, as the children were settling down in their beds, Velmarie led them in a prayer, asking God to send His guardian angels to keep the children from harm during their vacation—and especially to watch over little strawberry-blond Hays, the smallest of them all.

Early the next morning, before the others were awake, Drew and his nine-year-old friend quietly sneaked out of the apartment to run down to the beach. In their haste to be the first ones on the beach, they left the door unlocked.

While they made every effort not to wake the others, the early-morning activity on the part of Drew and his pal had been observed by the inquisitive big blue eyes of two-year-old Hays. Wearing only his diaper, the toddler made his way out into the hall, then onto a balcony. Frustrated because he was not able to see over the solid stucco railing, Hays wheeled a luggage cart next to the wall and climbed on top to get a better look at what was on the other side.

And then he lost his balance—and fell.

Velmarie awoke in horror at the sound of someone pounding on the door to the apartment and shouting that he had just seen a baby go over the balcony. Her heart racing in fear, she jumped out of bed, and ran to the balcony. Taking a deep breath and saying a brief prayer of hope, she looked over the railing. Hays lay very still at least 80 feet below.

Velmarie is a nurse, so she knew that there was no way her beloved two-year-old son could have survived such a fall. Yet, at the same time, the powerful mother instinct within her breast continued praying all the way down the elevator that somehow God would grant a miracle and save little Hays.

When she rushed out onto the parking lot, she was stunned, amazed, overjoyed to see that Hays was sitting up, crying, moving—very much alive.

Somehow little Hays had landed directly on his padded diaper, and it had miraculously absorbed the impact of an eight-story fall. There were little pieces of diaper all over the parking lot, but Hays appeared to be unharmed.

"Cart fall," he complained to his mother, who was weeping tears of relief and joy. "Hurt bad."

No doubt little Hays did feel some pain, but after the doctors at the hospital had carefully examined him, they announced to a relieved Velmarie that her son had experienced nothing more than a large bruise on the right side of his face and some minor scrapes and bruises. He had suffered no broken bones, no concussion, no serious injuries of any kind.

Okaloosa County, Florida, Sheriff's Department spokesman Rick Hord told reporter S. D. Hubbard that it was a miracle that Hays Burton had not been killed or seriously injured. "His Huggies saved his life," Hord declared.

Velmarie Burton attributes her son's miraculous survival to a much higher power—one that responded to her prayers of the night for a special guardian angel to watch over little Hays.

*I*n 1967, Brad Steiger issued an early form of a questionnaire designed to gather information regarding the mystical and paranormal experiences of his readers. The survey would evolve over the years, and in 1987, it would be combined with a similar analytical questionnaire that had been created in 1970 by Sherry Hansen when she was a counselor at the State University of New York at Stonybrook. Now, thirty-five years from the survey's first distribution, more than 30,000 people from around the world have responded to its request for personal data and have supplied thousands of moving, inspirational stories. The following account is one of them.

In January 1994, Marvel Barrick left her home in rural Kansas to travel to northern Michigan for the funeral of her aunt Thelma, leaving her husband, Doug, and twins, Dennis and Dorothy, on the farm.

"Doug felt he should accompany me," Marvel wrote in her report for the questionnaire. "But we were still keeping quite a few head of cattle and other livestock at that time, and it was just about impossible to get anyone who would watch your stock in the winter while you went away. And if there should come any blizzards, then someone just had to go out and bring the herd into the safety of the sheds and see that every other cow, pig, chicken, and duck got feed and shelter."

Also, Marvel pointed out, the twins were only four years old and weren't "the greatest of travelers on long trips." Plus they had never been on an airliner before, and she didn't want to tackle that chore for the first time without Doug.

Marvel had intended to stay away for only a couple of days, but then unwelcome blizzard conditions at both the Michigan and Kansas airports made travel hazardous and out of the question. Doug told her over the telephone that she should just make the best of her time away from the farm and spend some quality time with her mother and sister in Michigan. He promised that he and the twins were doing just fine amid the snowbanks, and that his younger brother Chet was helping with the livestock after he had gotten stranded there on a visit home from college.

"With my mind as much at peace as a mother's can ever be when she's away from her family, I decided to take Doug's advice and enjoy a nice visit with my sister Crystal and my mom," Marvel said. "The first night we sat up and talked and reminisced, laughed and cried, until two o'clock in the morning."

The next evening, with cups of extra-strong coffee and a generous supply of Crystal's homemade pastries to shore them up, the ladies were still talking around the fireplace at 3:00 A.M. when Marvel suddenly jumped up from her chair to shout that she smelled smoke.

"Of course, you do, honey," her mother chuckled. "We just put another log on the fire."

Marvel insisted that it wasn't smoke from the hickory firewood that she smelled. "It's that horrible, acrid kind of smell that you get with rubber or cloth or electrical wires," she said. "I'm checking it out. Mom, we don't want your new place to burn up."

A few years after the death of Marvel's father, her mother had moved from the family's old five-bedroom home into a comfortable apartment, so it didn't take long for Marvel, accompanied by her obliging sister and mother, to investigate each room and declare it free of smoke and fire.

But Marvel simply couldn't get the awful smell out of her nostrils.

"Then all at once I was overcome with this terrible feeling of fear for Doug and the twins back on the farm," Marvel said. "Suddenly I knew with all my being that there was a fire in our farmhouse."

It was a few minutes after three—two in Kansas— but Marvel went right to the telephone and dialed her home number. Better to awaken Doug from a sound sleep and grumpily be told that nothing was wrong than to take a chance that her intuition was correct and have her family perish in a fire.

The telephone rang and rang. Four, five, six rings.

"The smell in my nostrils was getting stronger. I was nearly overcome with nausea and lightheadedness," Marvel recalled. "Why wasn't anyone answering?"

Marvel hung up. Ignoring her sister's and mother's assurances that everyone was sound asleep there in Kansas and everything was all right, she dialed again and let it ring.

At last she heard the receiver being lifted, then dropped, then lifted again. Her heart sank when she heard little Dennis coughing. "Hello, this is the Barrick residence," he said, repeating the salutation he had been taught.

"Honey, it's Mommy. Is everything all right? Are you all right, Honey?"

Dennis coughed again, then, his voice rising in fear, he began to cry. "Mommy, Mommy! There is smoke, lots of smoke!"

Marvel told her four-year-old son not to be afraid. "Go wake up Daddy. Go wake up Uncle Chet. Tell them about the smoke. Can you do that right away?"

Dennis coughed, then said that he could.

"Then hang up the telephone, honey. Go wake them—and tell them to call me back!"

Crystal and her mother prayed with Marvel during an excruciatingly long twenty-six minutes before the telephone rang. She breathed a silent prayer of thanks when she heard Doug's calm voice.

"I always knew you had some kind of superpowers, sweetheart," Doug chuckled, "but I didn't know they extended to your power of smell."

Uncle Chet had pulled Dennis and Dorothy on a sled while he did chores, and later, when they were back inside, he had set their wet mittens and his leather gloves on the wood box near the old cookstove that they kept fired up out on the porch to help heat the house during the winter months. Sometime during the night, a spark had popped out of the stove and landed on one of the woolen mittens. The mittens and gloves had smoldered until they had burst into flame and fallen into the kindling in the wood box. Although the wood had burned and smoked up the house, the metal box had managed to contain the flames until little Dennis had been awakened by his mother's telephone call.

"Probably about another ten or fifteen minutes and furniture and things near the blazing woodbox would have caught fire and this story would have had a very unhappy ending," Marvel said, concluding her account. "I went to bed that night relieved that no real harm had been done to our farm home, but I know if I hadn't somehow smelled smoke where there was none and called home, the house could have burned to the ground with my loved ones inside. Ever since that night, Doug has teased me about my super sense of smell that could detect smoke all the way from Michigan to Kansas, but I just tell him that all mothers have such superpowers when it comes to their family."

*O*n November 30, 1991, Ronald and Ashley Hildman were returning to their home in Phoenix, Arizona, from a Thanksgiving visit with Ashley's parents in Sherman Oaks, California. Their kids, David, eight, and Rebecca, two, were sound asleep in the backseat when they stopped for gas at a small self-service station off the main highway. They had taken another of Ronald's famous "shortcuts," which usually ended up taking longer than if they had stayed on the main roads.

Ashley got out to stretch while her husband filled the

gas tank. As she looked in at her two sleeping children, she was suddenly struck with an extra warm ray of mother love. Dear God, she thought, how she loved those kids. She would do anything for them, and if anything ever happened to them, she didn't know how she would be able to cope with such a tragedy.

When Ronald went inside the station to pay for the gas, Ashley decided that she would get them each a soft drink from the soda machine at the side of the building. While she was plunking the coins in the slot of the soda dispenser, she glanced over her shoulder just as a tall, well-built young man in a dark blue ski jacket and jeans was opening the driver's side of their car.

"Hey, you," she shouted. "That's our car. What do you think you're doing?"

When the hoodlum grinned at her, made an obscene gesture, and got inside their car, it soon became very obvious that he thought he was stealing their car.

"No!" Ashley screamed in horror. "Don't take our car! Our kids are inside!"

Ronald ran out of the station, his wallet still in his right hand from having just paid for the gas. "Stop, you jerk! Our kids are in the backseat!"

The young thug accelerated with a squeal of the tires and drove away from the station, laughing over his shoulder at the two desperate parents running after the car in an attempt to stop him.

"I'm calling 911!" Ron told her. "The highway patrol will get that creep. He won't hurt the kids. He knows better than to do something like that. He's just after the car . . . not the kids."

Ashley could think only of her two angel babies asleep in the backseat. She couldn't wait for the highway patrol. And she didn't find her husband's analysis of the carjacker's motives reassuring.

For the first time she took notice of other vehicles parked near the station. She ruled out an elderly man in an old pickup truck, but she focused immediately on two teenaged boys in a four-door model that looked as though it might have undergone a little "souping up" in the engine department. Without giving the situation another thought, she jumped into the backseat and screamed at the boy at the wheel to follow their car.

"Go, go, go!" she shouted, mentally teetering very close to hysteria, her voice rising to octaves and volume never before achieved. "That louse took off in our car and our two kids are asleep in the backseat. Come on, come on," she demanded. "Slam that pedal to the metal! Go!"

The two boys looked at each other with blank stares. Then the driver, at a loss how to handle a hysterical mother who was slapping his back as if he were a stubborn mule reluctant to move, mumbled something unintelligible, punctuated his confusion with a couple of curse words, then roared out of the parking place and onto the two-lane blacktop that the carjacker had taken.

Ashley tried to keep all grim and horrid thoughts from her mind, but they kept struggling back in and shouting for attention. What if the teenager should lose the creep who had stolen their car and their kids? Would he hold them for ransom? Or, God forbid, would he consider them a nuisance and kill them? What if the carjacker was high on drugs or alcohol and he should lose control of the car and crash, injuring or killing David and Rebecca?

About four or five miles down the road, the carjacker pulled off the road, into a public picnic area. Puzzled by such a strange maneuver on the part of the thief, Ashley ordered the driver to pull in front of her car so the thief couldn't drive off. Then she jumped out of the backseat and ran to her car to check on the condition of David and Rebecca.

When she saw that they were both all right and both still sound asleep, she gave a deep sigh of relief. Then she turned her attention to the carjacker.

She yanked open the driver's door, grabbed the thief by his ski jacket, and pulled him outside. Although she was five-foot-four and around 120 pounds and he was six-foot-four and well over 200 pounds, Ashley's adrenaline was pumping so furiously that she began tossing him around as if he were made of straw.

"You idiot!" she screamed, shaking the big guy so hard that his arms flapped at his sides like a giant bird with clipped wings. "You stole my kids—and you could have hurt them. What were you thinking?"

At last the thug jerked his ski jacket free of the furious mother who had been throwing him around as if she were Wonder Woman. "Deuce! Charlie!" he growled at the two teenagers who stood in a silent daze beside the car that Ashley had commandeered. "What in hell were you thinking, bringing this crazy witch along with you?"

"So what were we supposed to do, Mel?" Deuce, the driver, wanted to know. "She just jumped in the car and started screaming about her kids and ordering us to take off after you."

Then it all became very clear to Ashley. The older hoodlum, Mel, who she guessed to be about twenty, and the two teenaged punks in the car were all in on the carjacking.

In a brief flash of memory, she remembered seeing a car with two young men in front and one in the back drive up beside the station as Ronald was filling their gas tank. The big guy who had driven off with their car and their sleeping kids had arrived with the two teenagers,

Deuce and Charlie. They were his accomplices in crime. Mel had pulled into the picnic area knowing that his partners were behind him—but having no idea that the owner of the stolen car was their passenger or that she would also be an angry, hysterical mother.

And now, as the grim reality of her situation fully dawned upon her, Ashley knew that she was alone in a darkened picnic area with three young criminals. And she was all that stood between David and Rebecca and any harm that might come to them if the carjackers panicked.

"Hey, man, did you see those two kids in the backseat before you took off?"

The question came from the one called Charlie, and Ashley thought she detected a tone of fear in his voice. Charlie was the youngest, probably not more than sixteen.

"Hell, no," Mel snapped. "And what should I have done? Stopped the car and let them out? Let this crazy witch and her husband catch up to me at the pumps?"

Charlie wasn't finished. "But Mel, you know, grabbing kids is kidnapping, man. I mean, that's a federal offense."

Deuce had been kicking at a clump of dirt with the toe of his boot, obviously thinking the whole situation over. "Me and Charlie said we would back you up stealing cars, man. Stealing kids is a whole lot different."

Ashley seized upon the moment of confusion and apprehension among the carjackers. "That's right, boys. Kidnapping is a federal offense, and it brings the F.B.I. on the scene. When they catch the kidnappers—and they always do catch them, you know—it's the death penalty," she said, with a sharp emphasis on the word "death."

When she had their full attention, she made her grandstand play, praying that she had the moxie to bring it off. "My husband and I are both cops in Phoenix," she said, lying through her teeth, narrowing her eyes, bringing her voice down several octaves from that of the hysterical mother. "I've got my .38 police special in a shoulder holster under my jacket. Please don't force me to use it. I've got a shelf full of marksmanship medals to prove what a good shot I am. And, boys, I just couldn't miss at such close range. And I'm so mad at you for running off with my kids. . . ."

Deuce and Charlie protested that they had nothing to do with driving off in the car with her kids sleeping in the backseat.

"But you are Mel's accomplices," Ashley reminded them. "You are as guilty in the eyes of the law as he is. You will all get the death penalty for kidnapping unless you act fast."

When the three carjackers asked in almost one voice what they could do to help set matters right, Ashley told them to get into Deuce's car and drive slowly back to the gas station. She would be following in her car. If they drove to the station, waited for her to call the police, and gave themselves up without a fuss, she would see to it that they didn't get the death penalty.

Amazingly, the three young carjackers did as she ordered. Perhaps her impromptu impersonation of a tough cop had been convincing. Or maybe they were just young enough and confused enough to obey an angry mother without putting up any kind of argument.

When they arrived at the gas station, Ronald and the station manager assured her that the police had been called the moment she had sped off in the car with the teenaged accomplices and that the highway patrol would be there at any moment.

Ronald was so relieved at seeing his two kids and wife safe from harm that tears flowed unashamedly down his cheeks. He had felt so helpless and desperate when he saw her roar away after the carjacker in the automobile that she had commandeered.

Ashley apologized for what appeared to be a

completely rash and irrational act. She admitted that, if her mother instinct had not been triggered so powerfully—and if she had taken even one moment to think about the possible consequences of her action— she probably wouldn't have done what she did.

Incredibly, two-year-old Rebecca was still fast asleep and had not awakened once during the whole ordeal. David hadn't awakened until his mother had regained control of their car, so his only question was, "Where's Daddy?"

Later, when the police arrived and took the carjackers into custody, Ashley suggested that their youth and inexperience—and her display of hysterical anger—had stunned them into obedience when she ordered them to drive back to the gas station and give themselves up.

Twenty-year-old Mel was wanted by the police in several states for a variety of thefts, including automobiles and boats. The two teenagers, Deuce and Charlie, had stolen the car that had been used in the attempted carjacking of the Hildmans' vehicle and had a previous arrest record consisting primarily of shoplifting and vandalism.

As one of the law enforcement officers commented while placing the three young men under arrest, they made their big mistake when they stole a car with two kids in the back—and aroused the wrath of a very protective mother.🌹

The names in this true story have been changed to protect the identities of the youthful offenders, as well as the mother, father, and children who survived what could have been tragic circumstances.

*A*mong our [Brad and Sherry Steiger] most popular workshops are those that deal with the healing and teaching power of dreams. During one of the question-and-answer periods of a workshop held in San Francisco, one of the attendees brought up a very common concern over the old folk myth that has it that dreamers who see themselves dying in their dream scenario will actually die in their sleep.

"For instance," the earnest woman who posed the question went on to illustrate, "I often dream of falling from a great height, like out of an airplane or off of a skyscraper, but I always wake up before I land. I have been told that if I ever hit the ground in my dream, I will die."

We explained that such dire predictions of death while dreaming are unfounded, but Adam Chenoweth, a young man in his mid-twenties, rose from his chair to share a most provocative account of how he believed his mother had once actually entered one of his dreams and saved him from dying in his sleep.

Adam told the group that when he was a boy of ten, he had dreamed that he had been walking down a dark street that was completely unknown to him.

"A voice called to me from the darkness," he said, "and rather than being frightened, I found it strangely alluring. In my dream, the night sky was filled with the rumbling of thunder and the flashing of lightning, but I walked on into the darkness, as if knowing what awaited me and quietly accepting my fate. Then, in the brief illumination from the lightning, I saw before me a large, dark, winged figure. I shouted in fear, but the huge creature smothered my scream as it wrapped its wings about me. And then I realized that it was smothering me."

In the awful dream, Adam suddenly saw the winged being from a perspective much higher up. Then he saw the dark creature drop his lifeless body to the ground and fly away, its terrible deed apparently accomplished according to some unknown plan.

"I could see my body lying on the ground," Adam went on, "but my principal consciousness was floating above, observing the scene. At the same time, everything was growing darker and darker. Far off in the distance, I could see a light, and I felt that I must go there. I would be safe from all harm and evil within the light."

But just as he was moving toward the light, he heard his mother shouting in his ear. "Adam, honey, don't leave me! Don't leave your mommy! Please don't go into the light!"

His mother's voice seemed to echo and reverberate over and over again. "Don't leave me, honey. Please don't leave us. Your mommy and daddy love you so much. You can't leave us!"

Adam recalled that he wanted to move, yet he could not. He wanted to answer his mother, but no sound could issue from his mouth. He no longer seemed to have any control over his body.

Dimly, he became aware of his mother sitting on the edge of his bed, turning him over on his back.

"I felt just a trickle of life returning to my body," Adam said. "I remember my mother hugging me and kissing my face. I was barely aware that she had been crying and only dimly aware that her tears felt wet against my cheeks. And then I fell back into a deep sleep."

When Adam awakened that morning, he was surprised to find his mother in his bed, holding him close to her. His father sat in his pajamas and robe in a chair next to the bedside.

"Mom told me that she had had a terrible dream in which the Angel of Death had come for me," Adam said. "She said that she had seen this dark, winged being clutching me to its breast, preparing to fly away with me. She had screamed and shouted at it until it dropped me and flew away into the night sky. In the dream, she had tried to revive me, and she said that she could see my soul rising to meet an Angel of Light that appeared to be coming to usher me home to heaven. She cried out to me to come back. She pleaded with me not to leave her and not to go into the light with the angel.

"At that point she had awakened and rushed into my bedroom—where she became horribly frightened when she couldn't seem to wake me. At last, I showed some signs of consciousness, but she stayed with me all the rest of the night."

Adam's father got to his feet and bent over to kiss his wife and son. Then Adam saw him jerk erect, his face becoming pale in the early-morning light. "Dear God, holy mother," Adam heard his father say over and over again. And then his mother sat up to see what had so disturbed her husband, and she could not suppress a gasp of concern.

In a few minutes, Adam could see for himself in a mirror just what it was that had so upset his parents.

"The skin under my eyes, around my mouth, and at the edge of my nostrils was bluish in color," Adam said. "My fingernails were blue, and so were my toenails and the palms of my hands. My whole body felt cold, and it was difficult to move. And my mother noticed a place in my right eye where the white seemed to have congealed."

After a few hours, Adam recalled, the bluish tint left his fingernails and his palms, and he regained the full movement of his body. However, it took nearly a week for the blue on his face to go away, and fifteen years later, he still had the bizarre spot in his right eye.

"Not long ago, when I was getting an insurance physical," Adam said, "the doctor examining me took notice of the strange spot in my eye. He said that I must have come very close to death at some time for such a spot to have formed."

Adam believes firmly that something incredibly odd and potentially life threatening occurred to him in that most peculiar dream of death, and that it was only the intervention of his mother that saved his life. "Her great love for me allowed her to enter that dream—or whatever it was—and drive away the Angel of Death—or whatever it was—before it lifted aloft with my soul. If it had been ordained that I was to have died in my sleep that night, the miracle of my mother's love was strong enough to change my fate."

*R*enae Dieterich's thirteen-year-old daughter, Christy, came down with a very bad case of pneumonia in December 1993. Because Renae's husband had been transferred to another city and was commuting home on weekends, and because she also had two small children, Renae had no choice other than to return home in the evening rather than stay at her daughter's bedside in the hospital.

"I had just started to drift off that night when I clearly heard Christy's voice calling to me: 'Mom, I'm dying. Help me, Mom! I'm dying but no one knows it.

I can't make the light work to bring the nurses. I can't speak. Help me, Mom! I'm dying!'"

Renae didn't hesitate to act. She saw no need to attempt a rationalization of the voice. She knew that she had not been dreaming, and she knew that she had heard her daughter's voice. She looked in on her two younger children, four-year-old Stephanie and eight-year-old Annette, and saw that they were sleeping peacefully. Saying a silent prayer that they would remain fast asleep, she left for the hospital.

It was after midnight when she arrived at the hospital's reception area, and she was coldly informed that visiting hours were over.

Renae sighed that she was well aware of the visiting hours schedule, since she had spent the better part of the last two days there. She insisted that they examine her daughter at once.

Again she was informed, in a crisp voice, that a night nurse had just looked in on Christy and she was sleeping restfully.

Renae could not be put off. She demanded that a doctor be called to examine Christy or she would run into the room and look at her for herself.

"I am not a small woman," Renae said. "A couple of the nurses who had heard the disturbance that I was making came to investigate. They took a good look at me and saw that I meant what I said. They summoned a doctor, who listened wearily to their statements and my pleas. Then, in order to humor me and get rid of me, he agreed to look in on Christy."

Renae waited at the desk for a few moments; then, provoked by a terrible rush of anxiety, she brushed aside a nurse and ran up the stairs leading to the corridor that contained her daughter's room.

She arrived just in time to hear the doctor's harsh whisper of alarm: "My God, this patient isn't getting enough oxygen. She's dying!"

Quick work on the part of the doctor and the nurses saved Christy's life.

Later, when she had regained consciousness, Christy told Renae how she had lain there knowing that she was dying, and how she had desperately sought to send a cry for help to her mother at home.

"Somehow," Christy said, tears welling in her eyes, "even though I couldn't speak or summon the strength to get help from the nurses, I knew that my mother would be able to hear me and come to help me—and she did."

*F*or those moms who would like to attune their spiritual gifts and allow themselves to exercise an even closer connection between themselves and their children, we now offer a number of simple exercises that may be employed to strengthen the power of the "magic glue" that binds you together with your children.

In an earnest attempt to offend no one and to be as ecumenical and nondenominational as possible, let us make clear to the readers of this book that they should feel free to employ their own individual concepts of God

the Creator in experimenting with the following
techniques. We will suggest that God, All-That-Is, may
in reality be an eternally powerful energy source, but we
completely understand that it aids us as human beings if
we visualize God as an individualized presence, such as
the image of a loving Father or Mother.

Many spiritual traditions refer to the feminine
creative principle and the masculine guiding principle as
the twin energies that compose God, the Source, the
Great Mystery. As Paramahansa Yogananda, author of
Autobiography of a Yogi, phrased it, the Divine Mother is
that aspect of God that is active in creation and that
represents the Lord's loving and compassionate qualities.

The feminine creative principle is thus often referred
to as the Divine Mother or the Great Mother, the Magna
Mater. For purposes of visualization, we will employ
such terms in a few of the exercises that follow. Those
who wish to practice these techniques may accept the
image of the Divine Mother or employ their own
concepts with equally successful results.

Connecting the Invisible Telephone Line Between You and Your Child

The invisible telephone line that moms were using
centuries before Alexander Graham Bell was a bouncing
baby boy on his mother's knee, is the ability to

telepathically tune in on their children wherever they may be. Here is a basic exercise to help you connect your invisible telephone line between you and your child — or children. It is best to sit quietly for a few minutes before attempting a telepathic transfer. Be certain that you have chosen a time when you are quite certain that you will not be interrupted.

First, sit quietly for a few moments and visualize the vastness of space. Reflect upon the meaninglessness of time.

See yourself as a circle that grows and grows until it occupies the Earth, the galaxy, the universe.

Now, visualize the child with whom you wish to achieve telepathic contact. See the child clearly. Feel the child's presence.

In your mind, speak to your child as if he or she were sitting there before you. Do not speak aloud. Speak mentally.

Breathe in comfortably deep breaths; this will give added power to the broadcasting station of the mind.

Mentally relay the messages that you wish your child to receive from you.

Ask your child to call you or to get in touch with you.

Practice this on a daily basis for at least fifteen minutes, setting aside approximately the same time every day. Continue this exercise until you achieve results.

Transmitting Healing Energy to Your Child

You may also send healing thoughts to your child when he or she is ill. You must understand, of course, that it is not you who heals, but your act of tuning in to the Infinite Mind that does so.

A word of caution must herewith be expressed: When you transmit healing energy to a child who is ill, you must visualize that child as being *completely* healed.

You must not permit yourself to see the child as he or she is at the present time, miserable in the throes of the illness.

You must actually see your child in the desired state of perfect health and *know* that it will be so.

Telepathically Erasing a Bad Habit

If you are concerned about a child who has a very bad habit that needs correcting, you may send mental pictures to your child that contain images of the practice in question that are so unpleasant and disagreeable that he or she of free choice will give up the disagreeable practice.

The same caution regarding the sending of mental images of healing also applies in this case. When you visualize a child who is plagued with a bad habit, he or she must be seen as triumphant over the annoying practice. You must imagine the child as having completely forsaken the habit. Only by seeing the bad habit as negated will it be discontinued.

The most vital point in telepathically healing or helping is this: You must actually *see* the desired condition and *know* that it will be so.

The Glass of Water Telepathy Exercise

Here is another easy-to-master exercise for developing telepathy:

- Erase everything from your mind. Forget all those petty things that are troubling you and relax your mind.
- Attain peace and calm. Achieve harmony. Do not think!
- You must release the irritations in your mind and banish from your consciousness all things that disturb you. You must tell yourself to become calm and peaceful.
- You must command yourself to react to no outside disturbances or distractions.
- Do not think! That is the difference between the way your conscious mind and your unconscious mind work. You must remain absolutely calm at the time your conscious is controlling your actions.

- Fill a glass of water and place it on the table before you. The glass of water is merely a physical object on which to focus your attention and to permit the unconscious to rise above your conscious mind.

- Stare at the water for five minutes or so and erase all thoughts from your mind.

- Do not think of a thing. Just look at the water.

- Once you have achieved the proper conditions, you will feel psychic energy and *knowing* build up within you.

- Once you have blanked out your conscious mind by focusing on the glass of water, you will find it easy to achieve the altered state of consciousness necessary for the transmission of your telepathic abilities.

Learn How to "Read" Objects

Psychometry is the ability to hold an object such as a ring, a necklace, or a bracelet and be able to "read them," that is, to receive impressions from them. The development of such a talent could certainly assist any mom to become even more insightful and gifted than she already is.

When you first begin to psychometrize an article, you should speak spontaneously. Do not hesitate to say exactly whatever comes to your mind.

There is no need to concentrate, or even to think hard; in fact, the secret to developing the ability to psychometrize—and to developing all psychic abilities—lies in just being spontaneous, immediately saying what comes to your mind. Sometimes this can be a little embarrassing if something of an intimate nature should come to you, but if you truly feel the urge to speak frankly, you should do so.

You may begin your exercises by psychometrizing for yourself. Take an object that belongs to you, something that you have worn or used for some time, such as a ring or a brush.

Sit quietly, holding the object. Do not force ideas or attempt to concentrate.

Have a pad and pen at your side, and as fast as your thoughts come to you, write them down. There will be times when you think, "This sounds impossible"; still, write it all down. Do not continue this exercise for too long a period, however.

By psychometrizing for yourself, you will find that you receive insights that can guide you in your daily life. Infinite intelligence can channel through you at this time.

Do not take credit for this information or become egotistical in your work. Remember the words from the Bible: "I, of myself, can do nothing."

The power that guides you will disappear if you

become smug and arrogant. You must remember that you are an instrument tuned to receive.

When you psychometrize for your children, you may tell them your impressions rather than jotting them down. To experiment further and to increase your psychometric abilities, ask friends to lend you their old letters from people whom you do not know. Request objects that they have received through family inheritances and the like.

Remember that you are an instrument. Permit the messages to flow through you in a spontaneous manner. Understand that there will always be a *knowing*. You will not guess. You will not waver. Never doubt your impressions once you learn to distinguish the sensations of the *knowing*.

Strengthen Your Mother's Intuition

You need not visit Madame LaZonga to have your fortune told or call anybody's psychic hotline. Neither do you have to sit around waiting for a premonition to strike you from out of the heavens. You can learn to strengthen your own intuitive abilities.

Here is an exercise that, properly and regularly practiced, can strengthen your intuitive muscles:

- Get a notebook in which to keep score of your

ability to predict according to your rational level
and according to your intuitive level.

- Draw two columns on a sheet of paper, labeling
  one column "Intellect" and the other "Intuition."
- Now, sit, lie, or assume a comfortable meditative
  posture of complete relaxation. Use your rational
  mental processes to make an intelligent
  prediction about the following future possibilities:

1. A request, remark, or statement that your
   child will make the next time you see him
   or her.
2. Two events that will occur at your home
   involving your children—one event negative,
   the other positive.
3. Two events that will occur to your children
   away from the home—one negative, the other
   positive.
4. Seeing or hearing from a person with whom
   you have not had contact for a long period
   of time.

- After you have made these intelligent guesses,
  be certain that they are all recorded in your
  "Intellect" column.
- Now, as completely as possible, permit yourself

to enter an altered state of awareness, a
daydreaming, trancelike state. Clear your brain
of all distractions. Imagine before you a blank
white screen and permit images to form.

1. Imagine what comment or request your
   children will make the very next time that
   you see them.
2. Imagine two events that will occur to your
   children in your home—one negative, the
   other positive.
3. Imagine two events that will occur to your
   children outside of your home—one negative,
   the other positive.
4. Imagine a person you will soon see or hear
   from with whom you have not had contact for
   a long period of time.

- Record these meditative image predictions
  under your "Intuition" column and give both
  columns about one week to be fulfilled. The time
  allotted may need to be adjusted somewhat
  depending upon the ages and the proximity of
  your children.
- Remember also to record predictive images that
  may come to you in dreams.

At the end of the week or the time limit you allotted, mark the outcome of the number of foreseen events that came true. See if you predict better by hunches through your intuition or by reliance on your intellectual processes. If both columns correspond to a large degree, you may have learned to develop an excellent bridge between your psychic and your mental abilities.

Reading Tomorrow's Newspaper Today

Here is a supplementary exercise using the daily newspaper as a tool to improve your precognitive ability:

1. Note the major political events in the newspaper. Attempt to predict their outcomes by both the "Intellect" and the "Intuitive" methods.
2. Try to predict by both methods the subject matter and the exact wording of the major headlines in tomorrow's newspaper.
3. Foresee who will be in the most important pictures in tomorrow's newspaper—men, women, children, celebrities, politicians—and envision what they will be doing.

You may wish to conduct these exercises with a friend or a relative so that the two of you can cross-check one another. Continue these techniques for a month. The serious student will keep a running diary in order to obtain the most desirable results.

A Final Tip: So often those people who are just beginning to develop their ESP (extra sensory perception) abilities expect to *see* clear and distinct images at once. Sometimes, especially when you are just beginning, you will *feel* rather than see something. You will *feel* that your daughter is trying to contact you. You will *feel* that your son should not board that particular airplane and take that particular flight. Seeing often comes later, after your psychic "muscles" have become better developed.

Holding On to a Dream Message or Teaching

There may be occasions when you will awaken in the night and know that you have been receiving messages or teachings in your dream that have been transmitted to you by a higher intelligence. You may feel distressed when you become aware that you are unable to retain the full importance and meaning of the dream.

- Do not become angry or frustrated with yourself for having permitted the great lesson or urgent message to be lost to your waking consciousness. Call out to your guide or your angel to help you recover the full understanding of that information or warning that the Source wishes you to know. Ask that you receive again the full power of the vision that has just been transmitted to you.

- Take three comfortably deep breaths, holding each for the count of three. Feel at one with the essence of the divine that will blend with you.

- Visualize a golden flame of Mother Love within your heart. In your mind, travel a ray of golden light from your heart to the Divine Mother, the feminine creative aspect of the Source of All-That-Is that exists above you.

- Feel yourself coming closer to the Divine Mother. See points of violet light touching every cell of your physical body as your golden light begins to connect with the creative mother principle.

- Begin to sense strongly a closeness, a unity with the Great Mother energy of creation. Feel your consciousness melding with the love of the Divine Mother and ask that the dream message or teaching be repeated for your good and your gaining. Eliminate awareness of your physical body as much as it is possible for you to do so.

- Visualize yourself holding open hands to the Divine Mother as if you were about to receive some object of a material substance. With such an image secure in your mind, allow yourself to fall back to sleep.

- If you should not be able to recall the dream message on that particular evening, awaken that morning with the resolution that you will reclaim it on the next night.
- Prepare yourself during the day with transmissions of love to the feminine creative principle of the Source. Then, before going to sleep, call upon the Divine Mother to send her blessed energy into your consciousness. Charge yourself to bring back the vital substance of the dream teachings that you shall receive anew.

Dissipate Disturbing Dreams

If you should awaken some night and feel that you have been bombarded with negativity while your psyche was open to receive a dream of guidance or inspiration, deal with the chaotic energy in this manner:

- Visualize your head filled with a glowing violet light. Imagine that you are focusing the creative energy of the Divine Mother principle through your brain.
- Expand the violet light, the highest spiritual vibration to the Divine Mother, the feminine creative aspect of the Source of All-That-Is that

exists above you.

- Feel yourself coming closer to the Divine Mother. See points of violet light touching every cell of your physical body as your golden light begins to connect with the creative mother principle.

- Begin to sense strongly a closeness, a unity with the Great Mother energy of creation. Feel your consciousness melding with the love of the Divine Mother and ask that the dream message or teaching be repeated for your good and your gaining. Eliminate awareness of your physical body as much as it is possible for you to do so.

- Visualize yourself holding open hands to the Divine Mother as if you were about to receive some object of a material substance. With such an image secure in your mind, allow yourself to fall back to sleep.

- If you should not be able to recall the dream message on that particular evening, awaken that morning with the resolution that you will reclaim it on the next night.

- Prepare yourself during the day with transmissions of love to the feminine creative principle of the Source. Then, before going to sleep, call upon the Divine Mother to send her blessed energy into your consciousness. Charge

yourself to bring back the vital substance of the
dream teachings that you shall receive anew.

Go into the Silence to Receive Spiritual Nourishment and Gifts of Love

Grandmother Twylah, repository of wisdom for the
Seneca tribe, said that the Seneca have four very simple
questions that served both children and adults as
guidelines for self-discipline and for keeping the "magic
glue" ever attached between mother and child: "Am I
happy in what I'm doing? Is what I'm doing adding to
the confusion? What am I doing to bring about peace
and contentment? How will I be remembered when I
am gone?"

When disciplining a child, Grandmother Twylah
advised, "Ask him if he is happy doing what he is doing.
If he is happy doing the naughtiness, he may answer yes.
Then explain to him what will happen if he continues.
Let him know that he alone will be responsible."

The Seneca have a marvelous way of allowing both
mother and child to develop psychically and spiritually
and to strengthen the bonds of love between them. To
the traditional Seneca, to "go into the Silence" is to
meditate, to realize spiritual love, to feel the rhythm that
blends all creatures into complete harmony.

As Grandmother Twylah states it: "[The traditional

Seneca] listened and *heard* the Silence; listened and *saw* the Silence; listened and *tasted* the Silence. He closed his eyes and felt the Silence deep within. The woodlands became his chapel; his body, the altar. In the Silence, he began to communicate with his Creator—and he received peace."

In the cosmology of the traditional Seneca, the purpose of going into the Silence was to establish a personal routine that would become a regular experience for spiritual enrichment in one's lifestyle. "The preparation for this solitary meditation is so important that it should be done as carefully as one prepares his or her food," Grandmother said. "Spiritual nourishment is the result, and it provides a guideline for one's very existence."

With such spiritual nourishment, the gifts of a mother's love can only grow stronger every day.

Other Titles by
Brad Steiger and Sherry Hansen Steiger